W0082754

New Paths to Success

Determining Career Alternatives for Field-Grade Officers

Peter Schirmer, Dina G. Levy, Harry J. Thie,
Joy S. Moini, Margaret C. Harrell, Kimberly Curry,
Kevin Brancato, Megan Abbott

Prepared for the
Office of the Secretary of Defense

Approved for public release;
distribution unlimited.

 NATIONAL SECURITY RESEARCH DIVISION

The research described in this report was sponsored by the Office of the Secretary of Defense (OSD). The research was conducted in the RAND National Defense Research Institute, a federally funded research and development center supported by the OSD, the Joint Staff, the unified commands, and the defense agencies under Contract DASW01-01-C-0004.

Library of Congress Cataloging-in-Publication Data

New paths to success : determining career alternatives for field-grade officers /
  Peter Schirmer ... [et al.].
      p. cm.
    Includes bibliographical references.
    "MG-117."
    ISBN 0-8330-3571-1 (pbk : alk. paper)
    1. United States—Armed Forces—Officers. 2. United States—Armed Forces—
Promotions. I. Schirmer, Peter, 1970–

UB413.N48 2004
355.1'12—dc22

2004005095

The RAND Corporation is a nonprofit research organization providing objective analysis and effective solutions that address the challenges facing the public and private sectors around the world. RAND's publications do not necessarily reflect the opinions of its research clients and sponsors.

RAND® is a registered trademark.

Cover design by Stephen Bloodsworth

© Copyright 2004 RAND Corporation

All rights reserved. No part of this book may be reproduced in any form by any electronic or mechanical means (including photocopying, recording, or information storage and retrieval) without permission in writing from RAND.

Published 2004 by the RAND Corporation
1700 Main Street, P.O. Box 2138, Santa Monica, CA 90407-2138
1200 South Hayes Street, Arlington, VA 22202-5050
201 North Craig Street, Suite 202, Pittsburgh, PA 15213-1516
RAND URL: http://www.rand.org/
To order RAND documents or to obtain additional information, contact
Distribution Services: Telephone: (310) 451-7002;
Fax: (310) 451-6915; Email: order@rand.org

Preface

Promotion and separation from military service have been intertwined for the entire history of the officer corps of the United States, but cause and effect have changed over time. Aside from periods of downsizing, the separation of some officers has always led to the promotion of others. Through World War II involuntary separation for age and tenure was seldom mandatory and promotion was based on seniority. As a result promotions were few in periods of peace; periods of war or expansion led to more and faster promotions. In 1947 the policies for promoting and separating officers changed significantly with the implementation of an "up-or-out" system in all services. With up-or-out statutory boards replaced seniority as the means for selecting officers for promotion. These statutory boards also became a means of forcing the separation or retirement of officers not selected for promotion.

The promotion-separation systems before and after 1947 both applied one-size-fits-all rules to the entire officer corps. With a seniority system everyone who does not separate or retire is eventually promoted; with an up-or-out system everyone who is not promoted has to separate or retire. The services can make exceptions to the up-or-out rule by selectively continuing certain officers, but selective continuation (SELCON) exists to add a few years to the end of an officer's career, not to enable prospective career planning for an entire community. The lack of flexibility afforded by an up-or-out system is one argument for exploring the implementation and outcomes of alternative policies. In an age of increasing specialization, the officer corps has a number of technical and functional communities for whom more flexible promotion-separation systems may be appropriate. Any alternative must still have mechanisms for separating officers who are not vigorous, capable, and performing well and for promoting officers who are.

"Up-or-stay" is often adopted as a shorthand means of describing alternative systems. More properly, they might be termed alternative career paths because a wider range of career outcomes, desirable to both individual officers and military organizations, could eventuate if less uniformity existed. The one-size-fits-all command path alternative tied to existing promotion-flow separation or retirement is seen as creating limits to military effectiveness. But what are the alternatives that might be considered?

In 2002, the Under Secretary of Defense for Personnel and Readiness (USD[P&R]) asked the secretaries of the military departments to suggest officer communities in which changed policies might be tested. The RAND Corporation was simultaneously asked to outline policies that might be tested, to suggest how such tests might be evaluated, and to work with the military services in applying policies to communities as the basis for tests. The demonstration projects suggested here and the means of evaluating them are results of our research. These projects have not been formally approved or coordinated within the Department of Defense (DoD). Moreover, legislative authority is needed to conduct such tests. This report serves as a basis for seeking needed authority and for defining specific demonstration projects with the services. As such the report should be of interest to military personnel managers in all of the services.

This research was conducted for the Office of the Deputy Assistant Secretary of Defense (Military Personnel Policy) within the Forces and Resources Policy Center of the RAND National Defense Research Institute (NDRI), a division of the RAND Corporation and a federally funded research and development center sponsored by the Office of the Secretary of Defense (OSD), the Joint Staff, the unified commands, and the defense agencies.

Comments are welcome and may be addressed to the project leader, Peter Schirmer (Peter_Schirmer@rand.org). For more information on RAND's Forces and Resources Policy Center, contact the director, Susan Everingham, Susan_Everingham@rand.org, 310-393-0411, extension 7654. RAND Corporation, Main Street, Santa Monica, California 90401.

The RAND Corporation Quality Assurance Process

Peer review is an integral part of all RAND research projects. Prior to publication, this document, as with all documents in the RAND monograph series, was subject to a quality assurance process to ensure that the research meets several standards, including the following: The problem is well formulated; the research approach is well designed and well executed; the data and assumptions are sound; the findings are useful and advance knowledge; the implications and recommendations follow logically from the findings and are explained thoroughly; the documentation is accurate, understandable, cogent, and temperate in tone; the research demonstrates understanding of related previous studies; and the research is relevant, objective, independent, and balanced. Peer review is conducted by research professionals who were not members of the project team.

RAND routinely reviews and refines its quality assurance process and also conducts periodic external and internal reviews of the quality of its body of work. For additional details regarding the RAND quality assurance process, visit http://www.rand.org/standards/.

Contents

Tables

Summary

Background

In recent years, DoD has increasingly focused on creating a more strategic, modernized, and flexible officer personnel system—in particular, a system that will leverage its human capital to improve organizational effectiveness while enhancing the quality of life of its officers. To achieve these goals, DoD is exploring a wide range of personnel management programs that promise to offer enhanced stability and flexibility for service members while also placing greater value on experience and maturity.

One area that has received considerable attention is the military's promotion system. Secretary of Defense Donald Rumsfeld has expressed concern that current promotion policies risk driving experienced people to leave the military too early. Echoing these comments, Admiral David Jeremiah, the head of the secretary's Morale and Quality of Life Review Panel, has noted, "We make it hard for people to stay."

At present, almost all military officers are subject to a policy commonly known as up-or-out, which requires separation from service if an officer is not promoted within a certain period of time (or selectively continued) or when an officer encounters established grade tenure limits. Of late, the possibility of eliminating or modifying up-or-out has been a source of growing debate. In order to consider the issue more fully, the USD(P&R) asked NDRI to design and determine the effectiveness of new career path alternatives. Specifically, we were asked to recommend alternatives to up-or-out that could be implemented on a limited basis as demonstration projects and then evaluated for possible wider implementation.

Up-or-Out or Up-or-Stay?

The military's up-or-out policy mandates that officers who are twice failed of selection for promotion within a single grade be discharged, retired, or at best allowed to serve up to two more years in order to qualify for retirement. The up-or-out policy is intended to provide a strong incentive for good performance, create promotion opportunities for officers in lower grades, and lower the average age of the officer corps. Such a policy implicitly defines "success" by promotion.

The up-or-out policy, formalized in federal law in 1947, replaced a strict seniority system that many saw as inhibiting military readiness at the start of World War II. Since its inception critics have said the policy is wasteful, results in senior officers feeling their experience is not valued, causes officers to move through assignments too quickly, and reduces the experience level of the officer corps. Instead of an up-or-out policy, many private and public sector organizations, as well as some foreign militaries, have up-or-stay policies that allow individuals to enjoy full careers even if they do not advance beyond certain positions or levels. This policy, which does not entirely preclude forced separation, offers lower turnover, greater career stability, a more experienced workforce, and possibly reduced numbers of accessions and reduced training costs. If achieved, such outcomes would advance DoD's efforts to create more stable career paths for its officers.

Formulating Alternatives to Up-or-Out

In order to help DoD consider alternatives to up-or-out, we considered a range of potential substitutes for, or modifications of, existing policy. The simplest option is to eliminate up-or-out entirely or to limit it to junior-grade officers. We also studied various policies that would not abolish the principle of up-or-out but would still achieve some of the same goals as an up-or-stay policy, such as broadening promotion zones (e.g., allowing promotion consideration over a five-year period) or allowing officers to choose when they are considered for promotion within time-in-grade milestones and other constraints set by the services.

Because changing a single policy can have repercussions throughout the career management system, we also suggest related policies that could, or should, change if up-or-out is modified. For instance, the services will require a refined mechanism for involuntary separation of nonperforming officers. Assignment policies might also change if officers stay in service without requirement of promotion, and new career paths may emerge—such as a "fly only" option for pilots.

Compensation and incentives would also be affected by up-or-out alternatives. With replacement of up-or-out, average time in grade is likely to increase at certain grades, as will cumulative years of service (YOS). More officers will reach the point where they are no longer eligible for longevity pay increases based on the present pay tables. Thus, we considered various ways to compensate officers during a demonstration project through existing incentives, for example, critical skills retention bonuses (CSRBs) and the Thrift Savings Plan (TSP), which could be used to boost officer remuneration. Further, in creating proposed alternatives for demonstration projects, we considered nonmonetary incentives, especially geographic stability, in addition to monetary incentives. All of these related policies played a role in the final formulation of our proposed programs and their target populations.

Determining Target Communities

Within the military's warfighting communities there is a long-held belief that up-or-out ensures the vitality of the force. Given this tradition and a general skepticism about ending such an established policy, it was a challenge identifying communities to participate in these demonstration projects. In general, officer community managers resist ending up-or-out, except for the medical and legal communities and for certain technical specialists, such as members of the acquisition corps. Those warfighting communities that were more open to the idea of an alternative to up-or-out currently face manning problems they wish to resolve. As a result, two of our policy packages for testing attempt to address manning shortages. The risk of such a strategy is that an up-or-stay program is viewed merely as a temporary fix to a transitory problem, obscuring the benefits of implementing it as a more permanent policy. We therefore offer two other policy packages that explore other benefits of an up-or-stay system: greater flexibility in managing the careers of highly valued officers and increased return on investment in training and education.

Although we have tailored the packages for a demonstration project to particular communities, they can be adapted to other communities and even to other services. Specifically, we formulated four up-or-stay policy packages focused on four communities of different sizes:

- Air Force: individuals in multiple communities
- Army: the entire foreign area officer (FAO) community.
- Navy: individuals in the Surface Warfare Officer (SWO) community
- Marine Corps: individuals across the entire corps

Our Approach

These four proposed programs (or alternatives to them) would be implemented as demonstration projects. Federal agencies have carried out a number of such projects to test prospective changes in the civilian personnel management system. On the military side, the practice is far less common but has the potential to become a critical new tool for military personnel planning as well.

The design of our projects varies based on the size of the program and the participant selection strategy (i.e., whether participants are selected randomly or are chosen based on specific characteristics). We propose that one project—the Air Force program—could be conducted as a controlled field experiment. Such a design is possible with a program of this size, and random assignment from a pool of eligible officers enables conclusions about cause-and-effect relationships.

By comparison, for our larger Army FAO program we propose a quasi-experimental design. Quasi-experiments require sufficient numbers but do not permit random assignment. A strong benefit of this design is that it produces generalizable results, although it is difficult to isolate cause and effect. For instance, if officers who pursue a nonpromotion career path stay in service longer, it may be hard to determine whether the cause is the new career path or whether those who are offered the new path have different external job opportunities or are more prone to prefer career stability.

Finally, two of our projects—the Navy SWO and the Marine Corps programs—are designed to be qualitative case studies. While the results will not be generalizable due to the small numbers of participants, case studies generate in-depth qualitative information.

Demonstration projects with experimental or quasi-experimental design should include three components: (1) a comparison group(s) that is similar to the demonstration group but does not experience main project interventions, (2) baseline data to establish the conditions in the demonstration group and the comparison groups prior to the project's start, and (3) a longitudinal design involving periodic collection of data of interest and that can be used for any necessary midcourse correction. Both during and after the projects, program effects can be determined through a series of comparisons between the demonstration and comparison groups in order to evaluate overall effectiveness. Case studies may also require baseline and longitudinal data, but there is little value in collecting the same data for a comparison group.

Our Four Proposed Demonstration Projects

The four policy packages we propose represent specific suggestions for ways to implement up-or-stay demonstration projects and address a host of career management policies related to promotions, training, assignments, compensation, and retirement. They also share several common themes. First, continuation decisions about individual officers would be primarily based on employability (performance in current grades), not promotability. The system would shift to "perform or out" (either centralized or decentralized) and away from "promote or out." Second, these programs would highlight stability, with an emphasis on longer careers, longer assignments, and less geographical change. Finally, these programs would minimize required changes to current compensation policies, using instead current provisions for incentive bonuses and TSP contributions to compensate officers for longer service.

The policy packages are designed as follows:

Policy Package 1: Field Experiment: The Air Force Effective Manning Fill Program. Several Air Force occupations, including pilots, have severe "effective manning" shortages. This package would allow the Air Force to retain a small number of O-4s and O-5s in occupations with low effective manning. Those officers in undermanned career fields who do not attend in-residence intermediate or senior service school would be randomly selected to enter the program around their thirteenth YOS in the case of O-4s and seventeenth YOS for O-5s. Participants would receive a four-year employment commitment with a major command. Continuation in the program is contingent upon continued employability tied to performance. We anticipate a program size of roughly 25 O-4s and 20 O-5s added per year, eventually reaching, at program maturity, about 450 O-4s and 280 O-5s, if all continue to 30 years.

Policy Package 2: Quasi-Experiment: The FAO Military Professional Program. Most closely in keeping with OSD's original idea for a demonstration project, this program would eliminate up-or-out across the entire Army FAO community. Officers would be promoted as needed, and FAOs beyond 20 YOS would require an employment commitment from a user agency to remain on active duty. The program would allow FAOs to serve up to statutory retirement age regardless of grade. The FAO community is an ideal test case for several reasons. First, it has high midcareer training costs, which means longer careers provide greater return on investment. Second, FAO expertise is hard to replace, as it comes from "soft skills," tacit knowledge, and personal networks developed over a long career. Finally, extending careers for FAOs will afford the community a valuable opportunity to explore different ways of managing officers' careers. Specifically, FAOs could receive training and develop expertise in two complementary Areas of Concentration (AOCs), for example, the Middle East and South Asia. The program would apply to the entire FAO community of about 1,000 officers.

Policy Package 3: Case Study: The SWO Specialist Program. At present, SWOs who do not screen successfully for executive officer (XO) stand little chance of promotion to O-5 and tend to leave before retirement eligibility at 20 YOS. As a result, the Navy is short hundreds of SWOs at O-4. These shortages, which are expected to continue for several years, are currently dealt with through bonuses. The suggested demonstration project recommends additional use of a nonmonetary retention incentive, geographic stability, which has different appeal. In particular, this policy package will enable a select number of O-4s per year who did not screen successfully for XO to serve in shore-based billets as "SWO Specialists," with incentives and opportunities to serve up to their twenty-fourth year. This program should address the Navy's need to retain more midgrade officers with sea duty experience while making available an attractive career alternative that allows for both greater geographic stability and an increased recognition of expertise. We propose a relatively small program of about ten O-4s entering annually after the XO screening point and five more annually at 20 YOS, with about 120 participating officers at program maturity. This number of officers is reasonable for a demonstration given the size of the cohort, the available job structures, and expectations for participation rates.

Policy Package 4: Case Study: Marine Corps Retention of Highly Valued Officers. While both the SWO and Air Force programs are driven by manning shortages, the Marine Corps and Army FAO programs explore how officer careers could be managed differently. Continuation in this program will be based on an officer's performance-based employability in a specific assignment. The goal is to give the Marine Corps greater flexibility in the career management and retention of highly valued field-grade officers. At present, commanders must go through a cumbersome continuation process to retain these officers. Under this program, a small number of valued O-4s, O-5s, and O-6s will be chosen directly by a command or agency to fill headquarters staff jobs (e.g., in HQ USMC or at Quantico) where their tenure and experience could improve organizational effectiveness. Although this package is the only one designed to be offered servicewide, it will also be small and selective, much as the SWO program, accepting approximately nine officers per year, which is a reasonable number given the size of the USMC and the available billets each year. Marine officers would receive monetary incentives commensurate with a longevity basic pay increase. They would also enjoy greater geographical stability with longer assignments late in their careers and would continue to be eligible for promotion.

These different policy packages are tested through different experimental methods with different populations. As a result it will be difficult to compare across packages, as would be the case if similar experimental methods with similar populations were used. Such a design is not feasible because of size and occupational differences among the services.

Next Steps

To implement these policy packages as demonstration projects, two steps must be taken. First, the services must formally agree with OSD to put such a project and its associated policies in place. Second, because demonstration projects involve changes to military personnel management practices, Congress must grant the necessary authority. OSD bears the responsibility for seeing that both of these steps occur.

We recommend that OSD seek demonstration project authority for military personnel similar to that granted to the Executive Branch for civilian personnel in Title 5 of the United States Code. This process should begin immediately, as the aim of the project is to begin implementation of the policies in fiscal year (FY) 2005.

Both qualitative and quantitative data are needed for evaluation of the programs and should be collected before, during, and after the programs. Interim analysis will allow for program refinement along the way. Evaluation should include analyzing expected resulting grade structures, career tenure profiles, accession requirements, and costs or savings generated. Results of the evaluation will provide guidance to OSD regarding program design features that would likely lead to greater cost savings, a higher officer response rate, or other desirable outcomes. More importantly, the evaluations will address the advisability of administering the tested policies more broadly or making them permanent. The implementation and evaluation plans will be specified in more detail once decisions are made about whether and how to proceed with the demonstration projects.

Ultimately these demonstration projects should provide a wide range of results, establishing the relative value of specific policy alternatives and requirements, such as incentives, selection criteria, and community impact. In addition, these projects may indicate the likelihood of support for changes to the existing policy and the level of satisfaction and quality-of-life improvement experienced by those participants.

Acknowledgments

The authors wish to thank the staff of the Deputy Assistant Secretary of Defense (Military Personnel Policy) for their support, particularly Colonel Christine Knighton, Mr. Brad Loo, and Colonel Jim Wilkinson. Additionally, officers and warrant officers in all of the U.S. military departments helped us to understand how officer careers are now managed and how alternative career paths might be implemented. At risk of overlooking some, we particularly want to thank Major General John Speigel, Brigadier General Rich Hassan, Lieutenant Colonels David Moore and Cassie Barlow, and Captain Gwen Rutherford of the Air Force; Lieutenant Colonel Shimon Stone and Majors Greg Branigan and Bill Redman of the Marine Corps; Rear Admiral Deborah Loewer, Captain Larry Watson, and Commander Cliff Sharpe of the Navy; and Colonels Mark Volk, Karl Knoblauch, and John Davies, Lieutenant Colonel Dan Adelstein, Major Donald Vandergriff, and CW5s Matt Wojdak, Andy Barr, and Al Eggerton of the Army. We are aware that the views expressed in this report will not be supported by all service personnel managers, but they were uniformly helpful with their knowledge and advice. The authors also thank RAND colleagues Sarah Hunter and Ralph Masi for their insightful reviews of this report.

Abbreviations

ACP	Aviator Continuation Pay
AF	Air Force
AFEES	Armed Forces Entrance and Examining Station
AFSC	Air Force Specialty Code
AIT	Advanced Individual Training
ALC	Air Logistics Center
AOC	Area of Concentration
CFD	career field designation
CSRB	critical skills retention bonus
DA	Department of the Army
DMDC	Defense Manpower Data Center
DoD	Department of Defense
DOPMA	Defense Officer Personnel Management Act
DP	Directorate of Personnel
DS	Directorate of Distribution
FAO	foreign area officer
FY	fiscal year
GED	general education diploma
GS	General Schedule
HQ USAF	Headquarters of the U.S. Air Force
MAJCOM	major command
MORE	Multiple Option Recruiting Experiment
MOS	military occupational specialty
MRDEC	Missile Research, Development, and Engineering Center

MRMC	Medical Research and Materiel Command
NDRI	National Defense Research Institute
NRL	Naval Research Laboratory
OPM	Office of Personnel Management
OSD	Office of the Secretary of Defense
PME	professional military education
POPA	Personnel Office Productivity Analysis
RIF	reduction in force
S&T	Science and Technology (as in Science and Technology Reinvention Laboratories)
SELCON	selective continuation
SES	senior executive service
SWO	surface warfare officer
TSP	Thrift Savings Plan
USD(P&R)	Under Secretary of Defense (Personnel and Readiness)
USMC	U.S. Marine Corps
VEAP	Veteran's Educational Assistance Program
XO	executive officer
YOS	year(s) of service

CHAPTER ONE

Introduction

The Department of Defense's (DoD's) Human Resource Strategy is designed to tie military human resource management more closely to military missions and goals and the internal and external environment. In developing that strategy, the Office of the Secretary of Defense (OSD) conducted a review in 2000 of the officer personnel structures that result from current law and policy. The objectives for this review were

- to increase individual choice and service flexibility
- to make more time available throughout a longer career
- to value experience and maturity
- to allow seamless career flows
- to improve organizational performance.

The Secretary of Defense believes that one way to achieve these goals is to extend the length of officer assignments and the length of officer careers. In his view, current policies drive experienced people to leave the military too early. The head of the secretary's Morale and Quality of Life Review Panel expressed the same philosophy, noting, "We make it hard for people to stay."[1]

In response to these concerns, the Under Secretary of Defense for Personnel and Readiness (USD[P&R]) chartered research and studies to support transformational change of the officer corps. As part of these

---

[1] ADM David Jeremiah, "Special DoD News Briefing on Morale and Quality of Life," United States Department of Defense News Transcript, June 13, 2001.

efforts, the National Defense Research Institute (NDRI), a division of the RAND Corporation, was asked to design and determine the effectiveness of alternative career path policies that could result in longer assignments or longer careers. We were specifically asked to design alternatives to the up-or-out promotion policy that could be implemented as demonstration projects in selected communities within one or more of the services. However, OSD has final responsibility for the design and implementation of the projects.

The project complements an ongoing NDRI study that examines alternative personnel management strategies for military officers and builds upon our prior experience designing, implementing, and evaluating demonstration and pilot projects.

Up-or-Out and Up-or-Stay

Almost all military officers are subject to an "up-or-out" policy that requires separation from service if an officer is not promoted within a certain period of time and is not selectively continued or when an officer encounters set grade tenure limits.[2] Such a policy is intended to provide a strong incentive for good performance, create promotion opportunities for officers in lower grades, and lower the average age of the officer corps. Such a policy also contributes to a culture that defines success by promotion.

In contrast, many private and public sector organizations, as well as some foreign militaries, have "up-or-stay" policies that allow indi-

---

[2] For example, O-3s and O-4s must leave within six months of a second promotion nonselection unless within two years of retirement, at which point they must leave. O-5s not selected for promotion must leave at 28 years of service (YOS) and O-6s at 30 YOS. In general, O-3s can be selectively continued by a board to 20 YOS, O-4s to 24 years, and O-5s and O-6s for 5 additional years. Selective continuation (SELCON) was not part of the original Defense Officer Personal Management Act (DOPMA) legislative proposal from DoD and was incorporated during congressional consideration of the proposal. SELCON deals with the "back end" of the current officer management system by offering limited continued service to selected individuals given promotion failure. Up-or-stay is different because it is a prospective ("front end") alternative career path that is success oriented by other measures of success than promotion. We discuss this further in the next chapter.

viduals to enjoy full careers even if they do not advance beyond certain positions or levels. Up-or-stay does not entirely preclude separation for unsatisfactory performance, separation based on revised tenure rules, or forced separation if requirements change. An up-or-stay system will generally result in lower turnover (based on voluntary attrition) than would an up-or-out policy (based on forced attrition). Lower turnover leads to greater career stability and a more experienced workforce, which could reduce the number of accessions and training costs. In addition, up-or-stay is more consistent with career practices and expectations in the private sector.

Background

The military's up-or-out policy has drawn fire from critics since it became federal law in 1947. While the legislation was before Congress, Senator Guy Cordon argued that the policy was "wasteful and illogical for the technical services."[3] In 1976 the Defense Manpower Commission concluded that the policy caused morale problems and personnel turbulence.[4] More recently the U.S. Commission on National Security/21st Century argued that "the triple systems of 'up-or-out' promotion, retirement, and compensation do not fit contemporary realities."[5] Many individual officers have also argued against the up-or-out system.[6]

To understand why up-or-out is still policy after 57 years of controversy, one must understand its origins. Prior to 1947 the policy was neither up-or-out nor up-or-stay; it was a strict seniority system that could be characterized as "stay-then-up." The system had a pernicious effect on the readiness of senior military leadership at the outbreak of World War II.

---

[3] U.S. Senate, Committee on Armed Services, *Officer Personnel Act of 1947,* Hearings 80th Congress, 1st Sess., July 16, 1947, p. 5.

[4] Defense Manpower Commission, *Defense Manpower: The Keystone of National Security, Report to the President and the Congress,* Washington, D.C., March 1976, p. 261.

[5] The U.S. Commission on National Security/21st Century, *Road Map for National Security: Imperative for Change,* February 2001, p. 103.

[6] For example, Donald Vandergriff, *The Path to Victory: America's Army and the Revolution in Human Affairs,* Novato, Calif.: Presidio Press, 2002. For an older critique, see Nicholas J. Schmitt, "The 'Up-or-Out' Policy," *Navy Proceedings,* December 1979, pp. 35–40.

George C. Marshall was compelled to create a "plucking board" to remove officers deemed unfit for command,[7] and Dwight Eisenhower later testified to Congress that "not over five" of the Army officers available to command divisions and corps at the start of the war served in World War II. "All the rest…had to be replaced and gotten out of the way, and younger men had to come along and take over the job."[8] Thus, up-or-out became law as a solution to a specific problem.[9]

Up-or-out has been a career management policy for more than half a century now, and its corollary "youth and vigor" ethos is ingrained in military culture. Conventional wisdom holds that without up-or-out, the military will once again be burdened with antiquated or substandard officers. Many officers therefore see a very clear benefit of keeping the up-or-out policy. When presented with the possibility of changing or eliminating it, they ask a fair question: "Why?"

The easiest case to make would be that up-or-out has some obvious, first-order effects that the services find undesirable, such as a large number of O-3s who are forced to separate when they are not promoted to O-4. This would support Senator Cordon's argument that the practice is wasteful. However, the members of the line communities we met with do not believe this is happening. Some communities are paying critical skills retention bonuses (CSRBs) to reduce manning shortages; some fill billets by having very high promotion rates; all have the ability to selectively continue officers who are not promoted.[10]

---

[7] Forrest C. Pogue, *George C. Marshall: Ordeal and Hope,* New York: Viking Press, 1966.

[8] U.S. Senate, Committee on Armed Services, 1947, p. 1.

[9] Economic and social conditions of the day exacerbated problems created by the strict seniority system. For more than a decade leading up to World War II, the economy was mired in the Great Depression; with private sector jobs scarce, no one was about to leave a secure military job. Even with a stronger job market, moving to a civilian job would have been difficult because military skills were less technical and less transferable to the private sector. Older officers also were not as healthy as their counterparts today. When the mandatory retirement age of 62, originally set in 1862, was reaffirmed in the Officer Personnel Act of 1947, the average life expectancy for a male was 64.4 years. While nobody is suggesting a return to a strict seniority system, it is important to keep in mind the conditions that made up-or-out necessary.

[10] We discuss SELCON in more detail later, but it is worth noting here that it enables officers who otherwise would be forced to separate under the up-or-out policy to stay on active duty. In other words, federal law already acknowledges that the services want to retain some officers who are not selected for promotion.

Other contemporary arguments echo the conclusion of the Defense Manpower Commission 25 years ago that up-or-out causes morale problems and personnel turbulence. The 2001 Army Training and Leader Development Panel found that retirement-eligible lieutenant colonels and colonels do not feel valued for their experience and expertise.[11] The Naval Personnel Task Force concluded in 2000 that "within set promotion points, officers are required to fulfill more requirements than can be squeezed into the time available," resulting in shortened command tours and ticket punching in place of professional development.[12] Mr. Rumsfeld has said, "the Armed Forces make a terrible mistake by having so many permanent changes in station, by having so many people skip along the tops of waves...serve in [a job] 12, 15, 18, 24 months and be gone."[13]

The up-or-out policy and resulting promotion pressure is a root cause of these problems, but the U.S. Commission for National Security/21st Century was correct in identifying up-or-out as part of a *system* that includes compensation policy and retirement policy. The findings of the Army and Navy panels and the observations of Mr. Rumsfeld suggest that it is reasonable to add assignment policy to the system. If up-or-out is part of a system that has some undesirable outcomes, there is reason to believe that changing up-or-out in concert with changes to compensation, retirement, and assignment policies could be beneficial.

This Research Project

The USD(P&R) has asked RAND to recommend alternatives to up-or-out that can be implemented on a limited basis as demonstration proj-

---

[11] *The Army Training and Leader Development Panel Officer Study Report to the Army,* Washington, D.C., May 2001, p. 9.

[12] Naval Personnel Task Force, *A Strategic Human Resource Management System for the 21st Century:* Vol. I, September 2000.

[13] Remarks before the Reserve Officers Association's midwinter conference, January 20, 2003. Quoted by Rick Maze, "Rumsfeld Broaches Changes in Career Structures," *Army Times,* February 3, 2003, p. 12.

ects. The alternatives entail more than just changes to the law requiring separation or retirement for officers who are twice failed of selection; they can, and often must, address a host of career management policies related to promotions, training, assignments, compensation, retirement, and more. The alternatives are therefore packages of complementary policies. We were also asked to recommend one or more communities in one or more services where an alternative to up-or-out could be implemented. We have tailored the packages to particular communities, but they can be adapted to other communities and even to other services.

These alternatives will be implemented as demonstration projects, which enable introducing and testing new policies that are expected to provide beneficial change in a large personnel management system. The demonstration or test might require changes to promotion, compensation, assignment, and retirement policies in statutes and directives and could therefore require some combination of administrative and legal waivers. In addition, if the projects are discontinued, or if their policies change significantly, the original program participants will have to be accommodated as they continue their careers.

Organization of the Report

Chapter Two examines options for designing career paths that were considered in this study. We generated some options ourselves, but many are the products of our meetings with officers ranging in grade from captain to major general who are involved in personnel policy and management in each of the services. The meetings provided critical guidance for the shaping of alternatives to up-or-out and the identification of appropriate communities. Our discussions with the services focused on how officers could be used if they were to serve longer, who those officers should be, and which policies could be changed to accommodate longer careers. In the second part of the chapter, we offer OSD two options for obtaining statutory authority for implementing the demonstration policies.

Chapter Three is a general discussion of study design and evaluation. We present key concepts and considerations that drive decisions about the implementation approach and the measurement and analysis of outcomes. The real conditions under which this study will be implemented affect the methods for analyzing the programs as true field experiments, quasi-experiments, or case studies. Adherence to well-established principles of study design will help generate the strongest possible conclusions from the data and increase the potential to generalize the results to other communities.

An activity related to our consideration of study design and evaluation methodology was a review of federal demonstration projects for civilian personnel. Federal law grants the Office of Personnel Management (OPM) the ability to conduct and evaluate demonstration projects related to compensation, qualification, work hours, and other management practices for civilian employees of the federal government. We studied the design, implementation, and evaluation of several demonstration projects developed under this authority. Other models we considered include experiments that RAND has designed previously for the military, related mostly to recruiting incentives. Summaries of those demonstration projects and recruiting experiments are provided in Appendix A and Appendix B, respectively.

Chapter Four discusses the practical aspects of selecting communities where a demonstration project could be tested. Although OSD could simply ask the service secretaries to craft a demonstration project for one of their communities, we have attempted to identify certain communities that would be amenable to or appropriate for participation.

Chapter Five presents specific policy packages tailored to specific occupational communities, as well as prescribed evaluation methods for each. These recommendations to the project sponsors are not intended to foreclose the opportunity to develop additional policy packages for other communities or to modify the existing ones. Indeed, some negotiation or further discussion between OSD and the services is expected to put actual programs in place. These next steps are discussed in Chapter Six.

The appendices contain supplementary information on previous OPM demonstration projects and DoD experiments, additional analytical information, and suggestions for implementing authority.

CHAPTER TWO

Options for Designing Career Paths

Up-or-out is part of a complex web of policies that shape officer careers. The criticisms of up-or-out presented in Chapter One are part of a broader argument that the services require more flexible means by which to shape officer career paths and manage personnel. We begin this chapter with a discussion of current and prospective alternatives to a strict up-or-out policy. Because changing a single policy can have repercussions throughout the career management system, we also examine related policies that could, or should, change if up-or-out changes.

Implementing these alternatives, even among small populations, requires various changes in law or directive. Therefore, we close this chapter by discussing the relevant administrative and legal considerations induced by these new policies.

Current and Prospective Alternatives to Up-or-Out Policy

The military already has legislative authority to selectively continue officers twice passed over for promotion. These officers continue at their current grade and even remain eligible for promotion in subsequent years. O-3s may be continued to 20 YOS and O-4s to 24 years. In our meetings with different communities and services, we frequently heard that SELCON effectively means up-or-stay is already de facto policy, particularly when there are manning shortages. However, the officers we met with also acknowledge that SELCON does not eliminate the stigma of failure for those who are not promoted. And as one person told us, you cannot plan a career around SELCON. In fact, the argument that SELCON makes up-or-stay unnecessary can be turned on its ear: The fact that the services use SELCON indicates that up-or-out does not make sense in many situations.

The most straightforward alternative to up-or-out is to simply eliminate the requirement in federal law that officers who are twice "failed of selection for promotion" within a single grade be discharged, retired, or at best allowed to serve up to two more years in order to qualify for retirement.[1] As an alternative, the law could be applied only to junior-grade officers.

If eliminating up-or-out entirely for more senior officers is too controversial, there are closely related policies that could increase flexibility in career management practices, allow some officers to serve in grade longer, and reduce or delay the stigma of failure and the uncertainty of SELCON, while keeping the up-or-out rule. For example, officers could be considered for promotion three, four, or five times before they face mandatory separation. The number of looks an officer gets could even vary by grade—such as three for O-3s and four for O-4s and O-5s. Or officers could be allowed to choose when they are considered for promotion within time-in-grade milestones and other constraints set by the services. A third alternative is to move promotion points further out, such as 14 YOS for promotion to O-4, versus the current goal of 10 years.

These policies would not abolish the principle of up-or-out but would still achieve some of the same goals as an up-or-stay policy. They essentially broaden promotion zones and lengthen the amount of time some officers serve in a grade. Lengthening time in grade will provide officers more time for training, additional assignments, and longer assignments. Broadening promotion zones also delays the need for SELCON until later in an officer's career.

Related Policies for Mandatory Separation

The services already have legislative authority to hold "show cause" hearings where officers must make a formal case to avoid discharge,

---

[1] United States Code, Title 10, Section 632, Effect of Failure of Selection for Promotion.

but these formal inquiries are normally reserved for the most egregious cases. In the present system, the services tend to rely on the promotion boards to weed out nonperforming officers. The problem is that up-or-out also applies to fully qualified officers demonstrating satisfactory performance who are not promoted; the services use SELCON to retain such officers as needed.[2] If up-or-out were modified or eliminated, the services would need some means of pruning nonperforming officers short of resorting to formal hearings on a case-by-case basis.

Up-or-out could be limited to company-grade officers, with selection boards making more permanent retention decisions at some point between an officer's tenth and fifteenth YOS, which is when officers are usually promoted to O-4. By that time, an infantry officer will have commanded a company, a surface warfare officer will have been a department head, and a pilot will have been a flight commander.[3] Officers selected for continuation could be automatically promoted to O-4, or they could be promoted on an as-needed basis but without the threat of mandatory separation if they are not subsequently promoted. Nothing would necessarily preclude an officer from becoming a major before facing the selection board. Officers not selected for continuation would be discharged. This is similar to the practice of the British military, which has two key continuation decision points for an officer—one at 8 YOS and the other at 16 years.

Another variation would be to combine the functions of the promotion and continuation boards. When a promotion board convenes, it reviews the records of all officers within and above the promotion zone, as well as a certain number below the zone. Based on the board's decisions, officers fall into three groups. First, some officers are selected for promotion. Second, some are not promoted but are implicitly selected for continuation at their current grade—that is, these are the officers

---

[2] The services have told us that promotion rates in some competitive categories are currently very high, and separation for nonselection is consequently rare. Elimination of up-or-out for those categories would therefore have little impact. However, if conditions change and promotion rates fall, there will be more officers who are fully qualified but not promoted.

[3] One personnel manager told us that by the time a cohort reaches the promotion zone to major, the services "know who the good ones are."

who are getting their first look but are not selected. Third, still other officers are being reviewed for the second time and, when not selected, face mandatory separation. In practice, then, the promotion board already looks at a high percentage of officers and makes implicit continuation and separation decisions. Thus, it would be a fairly simple change to the current system to have the boards designate officers as promoted or *continued* based on performance, with all others separated.

While some service members have expressed concern that eliminating the current up-or-out rules would allow underperforming officers to remain in service longer, this alternative could actually remove them *earlier* in their career: Instead of waiting for these officers to be passed over for promotion twice, the boards could select underperformers for separation at their first review, shifting the emphasis to "perform or out" and away from "promote or out." Moreover, just as the services already have requirements for promotion, they could add requirements for continuation based on performance and other standards. For example, officers could be required to obtain civilian educational degrees and professional certifications, pass fitness tests, and meet performance standards to be continued in grade.

A different approach is to decentralize the process by taking continuation decisions out of the hands of boards altogether. Beyond a point in an officer's career, the officer could be required to obtain a commitment for employment from a command or agency in order to remain on active duty. In this report, we refer to this condition as "employability" and suggest it as a decentralized means for judging performance. The commitment could be written into a contract or structured less formally. The community or assignment manager becomes a facilitator between the officer and the command or agency, but it is the officer's responsibility to perform and to stay employable. The community manager would be under no obligation to assign an officer, and a command or agency would be under no obligation to accept an officer for assignment. Officers must separate or retire when they no longer have a commitment for employment. With such a policy, employability rather than "promotability" governs continued service.

Related Policies for Assignments and Occupational Specialties

Assignments both lead to, and result from, promotion. In the Navy, for example, O-4s stand a much better chance of promotion to O-5 if they serve as executive officers of a ship. Promotions can even lead to a change in occupational specialty. If a service overpromotes officers in one career field and underpromotes officers in another, some in the overpromoted group may have to change career fields to meet requirements. Clearly, changes to up-or-out or closely related promotion policies can have a significant effect on assignments.

With changes to up-or-out, the services could offer career alternatives outside of the command-and-promote path that officers follow today. The archetypal example is the "fly only" career for pilots. In one specific program we propose in Chapter Five, a small number of Navy surface warfare officers (SWOs) could be chosen as "SWO specialists" who would be recognized engineering experts who train ships' engineering departments as they begin workups for deployments. Entry into such a track could take place upon failure to select for a promotion or command assignment, or officers could self-select prior to facing promotion boards or command screens.

Rather than having dual paths within a single occupation, the service secretaries could create more competitive categories than now exist and specify which competitive categories are not subject to up-or-out. Appropriate communities for exemption would be those with high initial training costs or that require advanced education or experience. Alternatives in this area might be officers in new competitive categories at a certain year-of-service point. The Army has adopted a form of this. Certain restricted line communities in the Navy also access a large percentage of their officers as lateral transfers from the unrestricted line.

Elimination or modification of up-or-out, at the least, would enable officers to serve in assignments longer, pursue additional training and education, or compete longer for command assignments. Giving officers more time in assignments and time in grade will slow down some officers who, according to the Secretary of Defense, "skip along the tops of waves," and will increase geographical stability, which can be an important retention incentive.

Related Policies for Compensation and Incentives

Military pay tables are based on grade and cumulative YOS. For each officer grade there is a point after which basic pay does not increase. For example, O-3s receive their last pay raise after their fourteenth year of cumulative service, and O-4s after their eighteenth year. With replacement of up-or-out, average time in grade is likely to increase at certain grades, as are cumulative YOS. Hence more officers will reach the point where they are no longer eligible for structural pay increases based on the present pay tables.

If up-or-stay is widely implemented and the compensation and retirement systems are not radically changed, the pay tables will likely require greater longevity increases within grades for longer cumulative YOS or pay banding of multiple grades so that officers who choose not to enter the command-and-promote path but who perform well are not penalized financially. Any changes to the pay table will have widespread effects across all services and communities. For the purposes of the demonstration projects we propose, we explored means of increasing officers' pay for longer tenure without changing the pay tables. We identified existing incentives, such as CSRBs and the Thrift Savings Plan (TSP) contributions, that could be used to boost officer remuneration.

CSRB packages pay bonuses of roughly $10,000 to $15,000 per year, depending on the length of the contract signed by the officer. However, a CSRB can be much smaller (only about $2,000 per year, in the case of an O-4 at 20 YOS) to be commensurate with a longevity increase. The services also have the authorization to make contributions to an officer's TSP, which would be a financial incentive, but one deferred to retirement.

Nonpecuniary incentives are also available. As noted above, geographical stability is important to some officers, particularly those with families. All officers remain eligible for promotion while on active duty, which is itself an incentive for performance. Although it is unlikely that officers participating in the demonstration projects will be promoted, if up-or-stay is implemented on a more permanent and widespread basis, there may be a number of officers who are eventually promoted later than they otherwise would be. While the demonstration projects are in place, OSD officials have suggested that participating officers not promoted could be offered "tombstone promotions"[4] upon retirement.

What Legislative Changes Are Needed to Test These Policies?

Although we aim to craft policies that can be implemented under current law, any effective modifications to up-or-out will likely necessitate new legislation. On the civilian side, demonstration projects are the vehicle by which a federal agency or organization obtains the authority to waive existing code—Title 5 in the case of civilian personnel—in order to propose and test interventions for its own personnel management system. This section discusses two different approaches to obtaining authority for demonstration projects involving military personnel.

One approach is to request specific adjustments to various sections of Title 10 that allow targeted changes to retirement, promotion, mandatory separation, and other personnel policies. We characterize this as "narrow authority." A second approach is to request "broad authority" akin to Title 5 provisions regarding demonstration projects carried out with civilian government employees as participants. Title 5 permits federal agencies to conduct and evaluate demonstration projects relating to civilian recruitment, assignment, promotion, compensation, and incentive bonuses. The law states that the demonstration

---

[4] Tombstone promotions historically were used to advance officers one permanent grade upon retirement if they had been specifically commended for performance in combat. Currently (e.g., United States Code, Title 10, Section 3962, Higher Grade for Service in Special Positions) academy permanent professors with long and distinguished service can be retired in the grade of O-7. The concept is now generally used to reflect promotions that might be made concurrently with retirement from the military.

projects "shall not be limited by any lack of specific authority...to take the action contemplated."[5] A precedent thus exists for granting broader authority to implement such programs. The law for civilian personnel can serve as a model for securing the necessary authority to implement policy alternatives to up-or-out.

Changes sought under the narrow authority approach are more likely to resemble the legislation required to make the programs permanent, if so desired. However, such changes are typically implemented on a long time cycle due to the program and authorization processes of the executive and legislative branches. Furthermore, legislation will have to wait until the exact policies have been finalized with each community and service and may not provide much latitude for changing a program once it has started. On the other hand, broad authority can be sought in parallel with discussions with the services to work out precise policy changes. This will enable faster implementation as well as subsequent changes to programs as needed. Appendix C contains draft language seeking broad authority, which should be refined by the project sponsor, OSD general counsel, and the services. The next chapter discusses evaluation and following that is a chapter on choosing communities for demonstration projects. Chapter Five will use options as discussed in this chapter to design specific programs to test.

---

[5] Specifically, Section 4703 of Title 5 (United States Code, Title 5, Section 4703, Demonstration Projects) addresses requirements for carrying out demonstration projects. Section 9507 (United States Code, Title 5, Section 9507, Streamlined Demonstration Project Authority) greatly diminishes the Section 4703 requirements for Internal Revenue Service demonstration projects conducted by the Department of the Treasury.

CHAPTER THREE

Evaluation of Policy Implementation and Outcomes

Within the federal government, agencies have carried out a number of demonstration projects to test prospective changes in the governmentwide civilian personnel management system. A variety of changes are tested through the demonstration projects, including modifications to job classification, hiring processes, compensation policy, employee development opportunities, and reduction in force (RIF) procedures. Detailed summaries of ongoing and completed DoD civilian workforce demonstration projects are provided in Appendix A.

On the military side some formal experiments have been conducted to test new recruiting strategies.[1] If pursued more broadly by the military, OPM-style demonstration projects could be a critical tool for military personnel planning as well. Specifically, as these projects are designed to address organizational needs and problems in human resource management, they could be a valuable means by which to evaluate alternatives to the up-or-out system. As discussed in Chapters One and Two, demonstration projects involving changes to military personnel management practices, depending on their characteristics, may necessitate congressional action.

Demonstration Project Design

There are at least three options for the design of a demonstration project in the current context—a field experiment, a quasi-experiment, or

---

[1] See Appendix B for summaries of recruiting studies in which RAND participated.

a qualitative case study.[2] The choice of a design depends mainly on the method of participant selection and the number of participants, and each design option differs from the others in the types of conclusions it permits. Due to their similarities we discuss field experiments and quasi-experiments together first and then discuss situations in which a qualitative case study is more appropriate.

Field Experiments and Quasi-Experiments

Ideally, proposed demonstration projects would be conducted as field experiments. Two main features of field experiments make them the most attractive option for a demonstration project. First, like laboratory experiments, field experiments allow for the *manipulation of key independent variables*. That is, the conditions of the demonstration project are manipulated by the designers of the demonstration and are not simply preexisting conditions or natural characteristics. In our case we would manipulate the career paths of officers in one or more demonstration groups by offering them one or more alternatives to the up-or-out path. Second, field experiments involve *random assignment of subjects to conditions*. They suit situations in which it is possible to assign individuals randomly to experimental and control groups within a defined population.

If feasible, field experiments are the design of choice because they are characterized by a reasonably high degree of control over confounding variables—variables that can cloud results and limit conclusions about cause and effect relationships. In other words, field experiments exhibit high internal validity.[3] In addition, because they allow an intervention to be tested on the same population to which changes will ultimately be applied, they tend to exhibit high external validity and are thus more generalizable than laboratory experiments.

---

[2] For detailed discussions of experimental and quasi-experimental designs in field settings, see T. D. Cook, D. T. Campbell, and L. Peracchio, "Quasi Experimentation," in M. D. Dunnette and L. M. Hough, eds., *Handbook of Industrial and Organizational Psychology*: Vol. 1, Palo Alto, Calif.: Consulting Psychologists Press, Inc., 1990; and T. D. Cook and D. T. Campbell, *Quasi-experimentation: Design and Analysis for Field Settings,* Chicago: Rand McNally, 1979.

[3] The ability to draw conclusions about cause is the essence of internal validity. External validity is the ability to generalize cause and effect relationships to other cases. For a detailed discussion of internal and external validity, see Cook and Campbell (1979).

A more common design in demonstration projects is the quasi-experiment. A quasi-experimental design differs from a traditional field experiment in one basic way. Quasi-experiments do not involve random assignment of subjects to conditions. Rather, participants (e.g., officers in a selected community) may be separated into groups based on the needs of the management system or based on their own personal and career choices, just as they would if the policy under consideration were to be formally adopted.

Quasi-experiments, by their very nature, have important limitations. They cannot definitively establish cause and effect relationships due to limited control over confounding variables. For instance, if officers who pursue a nonpromotion career path stay in service longer, it may be hard to determine if they do so because of the changes in their career paths or because those who are offered the alternative career path also have different external job opportunities or are more prone to prefer career stability. As a result of this limitation, quasi-experiments have less internal validity than laboratory or field experiments, which are characterized by a high degree of control over confounding variables. Quasi-experiments do, however, have important strengths. They take advantage of separations into groups due to organizational or individual factors and, due to the relatively realistic conditions under which they are conducted, they are usually more generalizable than laboratory experiments.

Measurement of Dependent Variables. Both field experiments and quasi-experiments involve the measurement of dependent variables, or outcomes. Selection of specific outcome measures will depend on the goals and implementation details of the demonstration. In general, data of the following sorts should be collected for the richest results:[4]

- *Quantitative (i.e., countable and numeric) data.* Examples of quantitative data include data in existing service databases, such as

---

[4] Guidelines from U.S. Office of Personnel Management Demonstration Projects Evaluation Handbook, www.opm.gov/demos/resources.asp (April 1, 1999).

numbers of officers in a given pay grade, and data on officer satisfaction with the newly offered alternative career paths expressed in numerical ratings.

- *Qualitative data.* Qualitative data can be a valuable complement to quantitative data, providing important information that is not easily expressed with numbers. Information on policies and procedures as well as officers' reasons for electing an alternate career path, for instance, might be collected as qualitative data.
- *Objective data.* Objective data are factual in nature. These data may be either quantitative or qualitative. Examples include data on accession and retention rates or documents describing new criteria for separation.
- *Attitudinal data.* Attitudinal data are based on individual perceptions. Examples include attitudes toward policies under evaluation (collected, for instance, as ratings on a survey or verbal comments expressed during an interview or focus group). They may be quantitative or qualitative.
- *Data on the accuracy of implementation.* We will advocate gathering data as part of a process evaluation[5] to confirm that the demonstration is being conducted consistently according to the design over time. If the conduct of the demonstration changes either gradually or abruptly during the course of the project, the outcome measures collected at different points in time will not be strictly comparable and will constrain conclusions about the effects of the demonstration. These data may also be quantitative or qualitative in nature. For example, they may result from numerical data on tenure rates or interviews with key staff.

Key Elements of a Demonstration Project

To generate the strongest possible conclusions, demonstrations with experimental or quasi-experimental designs should include three elements:

---

[5] For more discussion of process evaluations, see Peter H. Rossi, Howard E. Freeman, and Mark W. Lipsey, *Evaluation: A Systematic Approach,* Thousand Oaks, Calif.: Sage Publications, 1999.

1. *Comparison group(s).* This group does not experience the main project interventions but should otherwise be as similar as possible to the demonstration group. For instance, we might compare officers who participate in a nonpromotion career path to their peers within the same cohort who remain on a promotion path. Other possible comparison groups are a previous year's cohort within the same occupational group, or members of the same occupation in a different service.

   It is important to note that the choice of comparison groups is a major determinant of the conclusions that can be drawn from the demonstration. For instance, if the demonstration group differs from the comparison group both in terms of promotion opportunities and compensation structure, the effects of changes to promotion and compensation policies cannot be separately determined. Only their combined effects can be examined. Choosing an appropriate comparison group can also mitigate some of the potential confounds that might threaten the validity of the demonstration's conclusions.

2. *Baseline data.* These data establish the conditions in the demonstration group and the comparison groups prior to the project's start, thus serving as reference points that can be used to account for initial differences between the groups. Baseline data are also compared with longitudinal data (below) to assess the effects of the intervention.

3. *Longitudinal design.* Data from the demonstration and comparison groups should be collected often enough to detect important changes in the implementation and effects of the demonstration project. Such data can be used to make midcourse corrections or other decisions about the conduct of the demonstration. It may be appropriate to measure some outcomes more frequently than others. To avoid time-related confounds, however, comparable data should be collected from all groups at approximately the same time.

Qualitative Case Studies

Sometimes the context in which the demonstration will be conducted does not allow for either a field experiment or a quasi-experimental design. If the number of officers expected to participate in an alternative career path is very small, a qualitative case study is probably warranted. Small sample sizes are likely to yield insufficient statistical power to detect effects of a complex intervention. In addition, it is probably not wise to assume that outcomes observed for a few officers in a single occupation will be generalizable to their entire population, much less to other officer populations. An advantage of case studies, however, is that they can allow for more depth in the examination of outcomes for the population in question.

Anticipating and Evaluating the Demonstration's Effects

Because the demonstration projects described in this report will have real effects on the careers of military personnel, steps should be taken to anticipate these effects in advance. As described later in this report, we have begun to model personnel flows associated with project interventions and will use the results of the modeling effort, along with input from community managers, to refine the program design. As indicated above, periodic data collection during the course of the demonstration will also allow verification that programs are being delivered as intended and identification and remedy of any program features that lead to undesirable outcomes.

For case studies, data will be collected on the demonstration group's experiences and perceptions, but there is not much value in having a comparison group. Even with a comparison group it will be difficult to attribute observed or reported outcomes to the demonstration intervention and not to other factors. And even if such attribution were possible, it would be unwise to assume the small demonstration group would be representative of larger populations. However, for demonstrations with experimental or quasi-experimental designs, the effects of the demonstration will be determined through a series of comparisons:

- We will compare data from a predemonstration time period across the demonstration and comparison group to "net out" differences between the groups at the start of the project.

- We will examine trends in the demonstration and comparison groups over time so that we can identify changes in the environment during the course of the demonstration. An example of such an environmental change is a modification to personnel policy that is initiated outside the demonstration but that potentially affects participants in the demonstration and comparison groups differently. Another example is a change in the labor market that alters retention patterns for both the demonstration and comparison groups.
- Finally, we will "subtract" trends in the comparison group(s) from trends in the demonstration group to isolate the effects of the demonstration intervention.

CHAPTER FOUR

Choosing Demonstration Project Communities

In addition to defining policies to test and determining necessary legal waivers, we were asked to identify one or more target occupations and services. We structured our assessment around policy modifications that could be applied to one or more services overall, to one or more different communities, or to individuals. Each project was designed to be different in terms of the community or individual to whom it applies, and the projects could be replicated for comparable communities or individuals in different services. All projects were designed to be comparable in terms of meeting the desirable outcomes suggested in Chapter One and in terms of being measurable against criteria such as entry into the program, retention (change in continuation), career tenures (average length of service), experience levels (average experience for controlled-grade officers), assignment tenures (average time in job), and cost (life-cycle costs including accession, training, compensation, retirement). Moreover, all projects were designed to have a discernible front end and specific entry means and to not just be a change to back end policies. For an alternate career path to have a chance of success depends on the ability of the officer in it to look ahead and plan ahead. The front end (as well as the back end) has to change for a career path to be considered planned. Ultimately, the research team chose one project in each service that we believed fit well with that service's or community's needs to suggest to our sponsor, and the rationale is discussed in this chapter.

Many accept the logic of doing away with up-or-out for members of certain professions, such as doctors and lawyers, and for certain specialists, such as those in the acquisition corps. The military makes large investments in the accession, training, or education of such officers, making them expensive to replace. These career fields are also less physically demanding and are similar to civilian professions where people remain capable and competent long into their careers. Our research sponsor was less concerned with these professions.

For the warfighting communities, however, the youth and vigor argument holds sway. As we explained in Chapter One, up-or-out was implemented to address some very specific problems the military faced at the outset of World War II, and a widespread (but not unanimous) belief is that without up-or-out those problems will return. Furthermore, people in conservative organizations such as the armed forces are probably more inclined to observe the precept that one should not fix what is not broken. So lacking prima facie evidence that up-or-out is causing many officers to separate sooner than either they or the services desire, we did not find many communities willing to participate in a demonstration project.

Those that were open to the idea of an alternative to up-or-out or at least were willing to provide some guidance as we shaped specific policy packages typically did so because they have manning problems they wish to address. Two policy packages presented in the next chapter—one for the Navy's SWOs and one for Air Force line communities—attempt to address manning shortages. Officers from some other communities believed that an up-or-stay demonstration program would have no effect on manning shortages because of the pull of high-paying private sector jobs. One such example is the Army's Special Forces warrant officers.

As a practical matter it was easier to get cooperation from a community if it had a manning shortage. The risk of such a strategy is that an up-or-stay program then becomes a fix to a temporary problem and the benefits of implementing it as a more permanent policy could be ignored. We therefore offer two other policy packages, one for the Marines and one for Army foreign area officers (FAOs), that explore other benefits of an up-or-stay system: greater flexibility in managing the careers of highly valued officers and increased return on investment in training and education.

The specific policy packages for Navy SWOs, Army FAOs, the Air Force, and the Marines are presented in the next chapter. These are simply recommendations that OSD may choose to follow or to modify as deemed fit. The policies themselves might be changed, and we have already discussed alternative ways to implement an up-or-stay demonstration project. The communities or services where the policies are implemented might also be changed. Accordingly, we now provide some general thoughts on how up-or-stay policies could be applied servicewide, to particular communities, and to individual officers.

Apply servicewide. Modifications to up-or-out could be applied broadly to encompass an entire service. For such an expansive application, a demonstration project would be difficult to carry out. Such projects usually operate within a specific time frame and, if deemed unsuccessful, they can be ended. To undo a servicewide policy change, however, would be unwieldy at best. If up-or-out were eliminated servicewide, it would be a more permanent change in policy to be evaluated rather than a demonstration project. Program evaluation would entail ongoing monitoring of implementation and outcomes, but setting up the aspects of an experiment or quasi-experiment, such as comparison groups, would be more difficult. Probably the only comparison groups with some validity would be previous cohorts in the same service.

Apply to a specific community. For the purposes of a demonstration project, a participating community would ideally satisfy several criteria:

- There are similar communities in other career fields or another service that can be used as comparison groups, or there is a sufficient number of officers in the target community to permit random selection of one-half to two-thirds of them for the demonstration group, with the remainder constituting a comparison group (i.e., according to the current up-or-out system).
- Officers in the community only compete amongst themselves for promotion.
- A number of officers each year are not promoted and must either leave or be selectively continued.

- Training and education costs are large, in terms of money spent or years invested in development.

We have already explained that for practical reasons two of the policy packages we present in Chapter Five are for communities with manning shortages. However, manning shortages generally are not the hallmark of an ideal community for an up-or-stay demonstration project. This is not to suggest that up-or-stay would be deleterious in those cases, but depending on the reasons for the gaps, a demonstration project might not yield much in the way of observable results because the gap might be structural.

Apply to individuals. If an up-or-stay policy is implemented servicewide or for an entire community, the default assumption is that it would become due course: Officers not promoted would stay on active duty contingent upon satisfactory job performance. A different way to implement up-or-stay is as a much more selective program, with a relatively small number of officers exempt from the up-or-out rule. A pool of eligible officers would have to be designated, which in one sense means the program would still be applied servicewide or at the community level. But with a focus on individuals the up-or-stay program has a different look: It does not accept everyone who misses a promotion; instead, it takes a select group of officers who compete to enter some alternative career path apart from command-and-promote. A demonstration conducted at the level of a few select individuals would most likely be designed as a qualitative case study and, as explained in Chapter Three, would therefore probably not allow attribution of observed outcomes to changes introduced as part of the demonstration. Also noted in Chapter Three is that the outcomes of case studies may not be generalizable to larger populations.

CHAPTER FIVE

Demonstration Project Proposals

In this chapter we present four demonstration projects customized to particular communities or, in one case, to an entire service. The four projects directly address the four desired outcomes of the officer structure review discussed in Chapter One. Because changing the up-or-out law will have ramifications for other aspects of officer career management, these projects, including those discussed in Chapter Two, are really packages of complementary policies. The services and communities provided significant input and guidance, although none offered an endorsement of the projects, nor did we ask them to. These policy packages represent specific suggestions from RAND to OSD of ways to implement up-or-stay demonstration projects. Table 5.1 on page 49 summarizes and compares key policies from each demonstration project. We then provide a detailed discussion of the policies and evaluation plans for each separate demonstration project. We list the demonstration projects in order of scientific rigor (i.e., field experiment described first).

Policy Package 1: Air Force Effective Manning Fill

An Air Force calculation of "effective manning" for each career field measures the percentage of O-4 and O-5 jobs that are filled by officers of the respective grade.[1] Several career fields, or Air Force Specialty Codes

---

[1] See Appendix D for detailed calculations. The Air Force does not yet have a definitive approach to calculate effective manning. The approach we outline is being evaluated.

(AFSCs), have severe effective manning shortages: Pilots, for example, have 43 percent effective manning at O-4 and 35 percent effective manning at O-5. Others with low effective manning are developmental engineers, scientists, manpower, and public affairs. The shortages are generally due to low accessions and low retention in recent years.

The Air Force has addressed its pilot shortage by offering Aviator Continuation Pay (ACP) to officers who have completed their initial active duty service commitment. As the program is currently structured, officers through the grade of O-6 are eligible for payments of $15,000 to $25,000 per year in exchange for a commitment to stay for three years or more. Junior pilots are much more likely to accept an ACP agreement.[2] We have designed a program that targets midgrade pilots as well as officers in other career fields with low effective manning.

This is not the only effort under way to explore alternative career paths for Air Force officers. The Air Force is making changes to professional military education and assignment policy that are intended to give officers more control over their careers and to broaden the developmental experience of future senior leaders. The Effective Manning Fill program complements these goals by slowing the rotation of officers through some billets requiring a specific AFSC, thereby enabling other officers to serve in billets outside their career field. While those on the career path accumulate broader experience, those in the Effective Manning Fill program develop deep functional expertise. In the same spirit, Air Force Chief of Staff General John Jumper has written that the Air Force "will make sure that qualified people who do not pursue the command path will not be denied advanced professional development and a rewarding career to retirement."[3]

Program Overview
This program will enable the Air Force to continue a small number of O-4s and O-5s in AFSCs with low effective manning. Continuation of service will be contingent upon having an employment commit-

---

[2] Pilots who had just completed their active duty service commitment in fiscal year (FY) 2001 had a "take rate" of 58 percent in FY 2002. Pilots not already under a previous agreement or whose agreement expired in FY 2002 had a take rate of 27 percent.

[3] Gen John Jumper (Air Force Chief of Staff), "Chief's Sight Picture" November 6, 2002.

ment from a major command (MAJCOM) rather than approval of a SELCON board, which is the current procedure. The goals are to address the Air Force's need to retain officers in occupations with shortages and to provide a clearer path to longer careers for high-performing officers.

Criteria for Participation. Officers in undermanned career fields who do not attend in-residence intermediate or senior service school will be eligible to participate. These officers may not have been passed over for promotion to O-5 or O-6, but they are not on the command track and are less likely than their peers to advance. Out of this group a random selection of officers will be offered the opportunity to participate in the program.

Participants will work with their development team to find an assignment with a MAJCOM willing to offer them a four-year employment commitment. Officers newly accessed into the program will be assured of having at least one assignment. Continuation in the program is contingent upon continued employability tied to performance. At the end of a four-year commitment, the commitment could be renewed by mutual consent or the officer could obtain a commitment from a different MAJCOM.[4] If no MAJCOM is willing to offer a commitment to an officer, that person will be separated or retired.

O-4s will serve in their first assignment under agreement with a MAJCOM around their thirteenth YOS, and O-5s will serve in theirs around their seventeenth YOS. Retirement is mandatory at 30 YOS.[5]

Program Size. Each year 25 O-4s not selected for in-residence intermediate service school and 20 O-5s not selected for senior service school will be randomly selected from designated AFSCs with low effective manning fill. At the extreme, if all officers were to serve to the maximum 30 YOS, there would 450 O-4s and 280 O-5s participating once the program were fully mature. Currently, the AFSCs identified as having particularly low effective manning fills have a total of about

---

[4] As discussed earlier, the commitment could be written into a letter contract or structured less formally. The community or assignment manager serves as a facilitator.

[5] Typical commitments would last four years, although they could be extended to round out an officer's career. For example, a commitment could be lengthened by a year or two to get an officer to 30 YOS.

4,000 O-4s and 2,500 O-5s, which means program participants would represent about 11 percent of inventory at those grades and about 4 percent of all officers in those AFSCs.

Assignments. Officers will be required to have the appropriate AFSC and grade for the billet, but specific assignments will be determined by the agreements with the MAJCOMs. This could be an opportunity for the Air Force to accommodate The Pilot Who Just Wants To Fly, the archetypal officer who would benefit from an up-or-stay program. On the other hand, the Air Force might choose to restrict program participants to assignments in nonflying billets. There are about 240 operational staff billets authorized at the grades of O-4 and O-5 that can be filled by any rated officer. These billets are primarily with Air Combat Command, Air Education and Training Command, and HQ USAF. Likewise, there may be assignments in other AFSCs that the Air Force wishes to either place program participants into or keep them out of.

Incentives and Compensation. Retention bonuses can be used to provide additional compensation to long-serving officers who stay well past their last longevity basic pay increase, which occurs after 18 YOS for O-4s and 22 YOS for O-5s. The bonuses would not have to be large to be commensurate with a basic pay increase.[6] DoD contributions to TSP accounts would add to officers' retirement income. By law every officer is considered for promotion while in service, so there would be a slight possibility that participating officers could be promoted. Tombstone promotions (as discussed in Chapter Two) are also possible. As noted above, one incentive unique to this program, and even unique to a single AFSC, would be to allow some pilots to remain in the cockpit. That alone could be sufficient incentive for some officers.

Training. Participating officers may require periods of training and education to remain current in their fields. This training might occur during or between assignments. Thus despite the fact that officers must continue to receive employment commitments from a MAJCOM in

---

[6] Using the January 2003 pay tables, a 3 percent pay raise for an O-4 after 20 YOS would equate to about $2,000 per year; a 3 percent pay raise for an O-5 after 24 YOS would equate to about $2,350 per year.

order to remain on active duty, there will still be some opportunity for temporary duty training.

Impact on Community. There are several communities where this program might be implemented, and the communities may have some unique aspects in terms of career length, promotion opportunities, and so forth, so it is difficult to generalize the effects. Instead, we focus on possible effects on the pilot community, which is not only by far the largest of the ones where this program would be implemented but also, for obvious reasons, of particular interest to the Air Force.

The Air Force has considered making a fly only option available to pilots but has never done so. This program would be an opportunity for some pilots to follow such a path without the Air Force ever making it an explicit policy. If an O-4 is employable as a pilot and there is a MAJCOM willing to offer an employment agreement, that officer could enjoy a fly only career. Because of the requirement that the officer have an employment commitment there are no guarantees of a fly only career, but that could be how the assignments turn out. Alternatively, there are desk-job assignments that require rated officers. If the Air Force could lengthen the amount of time a rated officer cycled through one of those billets, it would free flying time for other officers.

Using the methodology outlined in Appendix E, we calculate low, middle, and high estimates of increased man-years for a cohort of pilots. This range of estimates is necessary because we do not know what participants would otherwise do if this program were not available. If it turns out that the officers selected to participate would have served long careers anyway, the program will have a small effect on continuation rates, accessions, and man-years served by a typical cohort. If, on the other hand, the officers selected to participate would soon leave active duty, the program effect will be much larger. A "middle-ground" estimate assumes that the participating officers would be similar to the rest of their cohort with respect to continuation rates—that is, some would leave soon and some would leave in a few more years.

The impact is measured in additional man-years served as a result of the program.[7] Because pilots represent the largest of the communi-

---

[7] See Appendix E for detailed calculations.

ties that would likely participate in this program, we assume that each year 20 of the 25 new O-4s and 15 of the new O-5s in the program are pilots. Our low estimate assumes all participating O-4s and O-5s would have served to 24 YOS and 28 YOS, respectively, without the program. With all now serving to 30 YOS, the low estimate is an additional 150 man-years. The high estimate is an increase of 570 man-years, assuming all O-4s and O-5s would have otherwise left at 13 YOS and 17 YOS, respectively. For the middle-ground estimate, we assume that participating O-4s would have had continuation rates similar to their peers through 20 YOS, when all remaining would have left, and likewise for O-5s through 24 YOS. Under these assumptions, man-years would increase 345 years. Currently, a typical cohort of pilots serves approximately 4,900 man-years between 12 YOS (about the time the participating O-4s would be identified) and 30 YOS. This number would increase by 3 percent to 12 percent, given the range of man-year effects we have estimated.[8]

One positive benefit that could accrue to any community is that as some officers spend more time in certain assignments, it frees others to serve in broadening assignments outside of their career field as they move along the command path. Increasing broadening assignments is one of the goals of the Air Force Senior Leader Management Office as it changes officer development policy.

Demonstration Design and Evaluation. The method of selecting Air Force officers for eligibility to participate in the Effective Manning Fill program allows for this proposed demonstration to be conducted as a field experiment. Random selection of officers from a defined population avoids selection effects that could otherwise make the results of the demonstration significantly more difficult to interpret. From an experimental design standpoint, first categorizing potential participants according to a few relevant demographic characteristics (such as years

---

[8] It is difficult to scale these impacts to the total man-years served by an entire cohort of pilots beginning with the first year of service because large numbers of officers enter the community after that point. Obviously, though, the effect of the program would be much smaller than a 3 percent to 12 percent increase in man-years if the baseline includes an entire cohort of pilots, rather than just those who reach 12 YOS.

of experience or educational attainment) and then randomly assigning participants from each category to the demonstration and comparison groups could further enhance the design. Such a strategy would ensure that the starting populations in the demonstration and comparison groups are equivalent in a few key respects.

Officers eligible for the program who are offered participation (based on random selection) and accept the offer will constitute the demonstration group. The comparison group would consist of officers who are eligible for the program but are not randomly selected to participate.[9] Additional information will be needed from the participants in the demonstration and comparison groups so that adequate methods to control for baseline differences between the two groups can be accounted for in the analyses.

Several types of data should be collected to support a process or implementation evaluation of the Air Force program. Information on the backgrounds of the officers who are extended an offer to participate can be compared to the stated eligibility criteria. Officers who are accessed into the program should be interviewed to verify that their development teams helped them find their first guaranteed four-year assignment. Finally, to ensure that effective manning shortages are indeed addressed, data should be collected to confirm that officers have the appropriate AFSC and grade for the billet to which they are assigned.

A main outcome of interest for the Air Force program will be effective manning at O-4 and O-5. Effective manning can be calculated for the demonstration and comparison groups separately and then compared. Effective manning for the entire demonstration cohort (comprising the demonstration and comparison groups from the same cohort) can also be compared to effective manning at the same grades for previous years. Other variables that can affect effective manning at O-4 and O-5, including accession rates, retention rates, and changes in assignments not related to the demonstration, must be tracked and controlled for.

---

[9] Other comparison groups could be used. For example, one could comprise officers who are eligible and offered a place in the program but decline to participate, depending on the number of such officers. Previous cohorts of officers can also be used as comparison groups.

Measures aimed at gauging officers' interest in and satisfaction with the program should also be collected. A simple and important data point will be the number of officers who decline an offer to participate. Those officers should be interviewed or surveyed regarding the reasons for their decision. Likewise, the rationale behind accepting an offer to participate should be investigated through data collection focused on participants in the demonstration group. For those participants, continuation will be contingent on employability. In addition to measures collected from program participants, a key measure related to employability might be levels of awareness of the program among MAJCOMs.

The exact design of the demonstration project for the Air Force will depend on a number of factors, including the specific measures that will be collected and the expected sizes of the demonstration's effects on those measures. However, one important feature of the design can be anticipated in advance. It is unlikely that comparison groups will be constructed that allow for isolation of individual aspects of the intervention (e.g., changes in assignments, compensation, training). Rather, the demonstration group will be exposed to a package of changes, and the comparison group(s) will experience none of the same changes. As noted earlier in this report, such a design precludes separation of the effects of different aspects of the intervention on the outcomes of the demonstration. It will therefore not be possible, for instance, to determine the extent to which retention effects can be attributed to compensation changes as opposed to the dependence of continuation on employability.[10]

Policy Package 2: The FAO Military Professional Program

Of the four policy packages presented in this report, the Army FAO program most closely resembles what OSD originally envisioned when this study was commissioned. All officers within the community—not just a small, select group—will be managed similarly to the way many

---

[10] Follow-up demonstrations that isolate the impact of particular aspects of the intervention can be considered if an effect is found.

private sector companies manage their professionals. The program will do away with the presumption that trained, experienced, fully qualified officers who are not promoted must be moved out of the way. Involuntary separation will still be possible for unsatisfactory officers, but it will no longer be treated as the logical alternative to promotion.

For a number of reasons it makes very good sense to test a program such as this for Army FAOs. First, officers are not designated as FAOs until they are at least O-4s, so the offer of continued employment for satisfactory performance is made to officers with approximately ten YOS or more, not to newly accessed lieutenants. Second, this is a community with high midcareer training costs; the Army invests two and a half to four years and an average of $50,000 in training each FAO-qualified officer. Third, FAO expertise is based on much more than training or language fluency. Much of it comes from "soft skills" and personal networks developed during in-country training, when an officer might attend a school overseas with foreign military officers and others native to the area. Friendships, trust, and cultural understanding nurtured throughout the course of an officer's career are surely more difficult to replace than a master's degree. Additionally, the foreign military officers with whom the FAOs interact often have longer service in their parallel role, and the indigenous peoples with whom FAOs develop relationships often have tremendous cultural respect for maturity. These factors suggest that replacing established FAOs with new, younger officers undermines the strength of the program. Finally, extending careers for FAOs will afford the community an opportunity to truly explore different ways of managing officers' careers in ways that could reap significant reward. Specifically, FAOs could receive training and develop expertise in two complementary AOCs, such as Europe and Eurasia, or China and Southeast Asia, or the Middle East and South Asia. This particularly makes sense in light of the fact that in today's national security environment, threats to the United States include international terrorist networks that are not confined to particular countries or even regions.

Program Overview

The FAO Military Professional Program will eliminate the up-or-out imperative across the FAO community. Officers will be promoted as needed, but those who are not selected for promotion twice or more within a single grade will not face mandatory separation or retirement. FAOs will be able to serve up to statutory retirement age regardless of grade, provided there is a user agency willing to offer a commitment for employment.

Criteria for Participation. This policy package will apply to all FAOs. Army officers will continue to be accessed into the FAO functional area and begin FAO training as O-3s and will receive the FAO career field designation (CFD) primarily as O-4s (or as O-5s and O-6s in some cases), subject to selection by a CFD selection board. All grade-based service tenures will be removed and officers will be allowed to serve until the statutory retirement age. Currently this is age 62, which would allow officers to serve up to approximately 40 years. After initial retirement eligibility at 20 YOS, the conditions for continuation will be similar to those of the Air Force and Marine programs: Officers must be offered a commitment for employment from a Major Army Command, Army Headquarters, or DoD for a period of three to five years. Employability, rather than promotability, will govern continued service.

Program Size. The program would be due course for the entire FAO community, which currently includes about 1,000 officers with the FAO career field designation. About 200 more officers are FAO qualified but remained in their branch in the Operations career field (these are officers who might be designated as FAOs later in their careers).

Assignments. FAOs are currently expected to serve a combination of assignments in-region, within the continental United States, and for the Combatant Commands with geographic responsibility for their AOCs. This policy will not change. Specific assignments beyond 20 YOS will be the result of mutual agreement among the employing command or agency, the individual officer, and the FAO branch chief or appropriate assignment officer.

Incentives and Compensation. Again, CSRBs can be used to compensate officers after their final longevity basic pay increase. For officers serving beyond 30 YOS, retirement pay could continue to increase by 2.5 percent of basic pay, and DoD could make contributions to officers' TSPs to account for the fact that pay increases will take the form of bonuses later in an officer's career.

We have already noted that officers who continue on active duty are already considered for promotion by law, and the FAOs will be no different in that respect. What sets this program apart from the others offered in this document is that it will be applied to the entire community and will therefore include officers who are highly competitive for promotion. To ensure that lengthening careers does not significantly reduce promotion opportunity for highly qualified O-4s, the percentage distribution of O-4s and O-5s could "float" while the combined number of officers in the two grades remains fixed. (This is a grade banding concept that is not unlike pay banding.) As officer careers are extended, we would expect to see proportionately more officers above zone in a grade, which could result in more above-zone promotions, a higher promotion rate for officers in the promotion zone, or both.[11]

Training. This program will enable the FAO community to explore ways to support Combatant Commands and other user agencies more effectively by managing its officers differently. With more time to cross train officers in complementary AOCs, the FAO community can more easily fill requests from user agencies, which typically come with very short notice. FAOs would still complete their training and FAO utilization tour to become functional area qualified for one AOC as O-4s. They could then be given incentives to become qualified in a second AOC, perhaps through the use of responsibility pay or critical skills bonuses or by making double

---

[11]   For example, the FY 2002 O-5 promotion board selected seven out of nine (78 percent) Africa FAOs in-zone, and one out of four above-zone. Supposing that this program resulted in relatively more above-zone officers, selections for promotion could have been six out of seven (86 percent) for in-zone officers and two out of six for those above-zone. These numbers are hypothetical but they illustrate the point.

qualification a required or desirable qualification for promotion to O-6. With officers' continuation beyond 20 YOS contingent upon employability, having a second AOC will also make it easier for them to fill a billet with a user agency.

In addition to having more flexibility to meet the demands for FAOs, the Army will enjoy greater certainty in reaping return on its training investment. Currently officers are accessed into the FAO functional area between their fifth and sixth YOS and subsequently begin training. However, not all officers will ultimately be designated into the career field as O-4s, either by choice or because they are in basic branches with shortages. Sometimes not a single officer from a "shortage branch" will receive FAO designation. Conversely, officers cross trained in a second AOC will already be FAO designated.

Impact on Community. Our modeling suggests the results of these management changes. The fundamental difference in the new system is that all officers are permitted to stay for 40 years of commissioned service. This longer service affects both the number of annual FAO designations (and thus the size of each cohort) and the rate and timing of exits from the community. We posit that the continuation of officers will vary by pay grade and year of service, as follows: We anticipate that few O-4s will leave the service prior to 20 YOS. We anticipate approximately 48 FAO designations at O-4 annually. Of the 48 officers in a cohort group, approximately two-thirds (32) will be promoted to O-5 at 17 YOS. Of the remaining O-4s, 70 percent of them will retire with 20 YOS. The remaining small number will serve until 30 YOS, when the bulk of them will retire, but a very small number (averaging less than one per cohort group) will continue to 40 YOS. While this opportunity will be available to O-4s, we anticipate that few O-4s are likely to remain past 30 YOS.

We estimate through our modeling that O-5s are more likely to stay for longer service. As many as one-third of the approximately 32 officers may retire at 20 YOS. Of the approximately 20 officers remaining, almost two-thirds (12) of them will be promoted to O-6 at 23 YOS. We anticipate that of these more senior officers, approximately one-third of both O-5s and O-6s will retire with 30 YOS, and that about 15 percent of each cohort will retire each year after

31 YOS, until they all depart at 40 YOS.[12] The result of this will be relatively small cohorts at each year of service between 30 and 40 YOS. For example, there may only be two O-5s with 35 YOS and around four O-6s with 35 YOS. Should this attrition rate be somewhat higher, the most immediate effect would be a change in promotion rates. For example, should O-6s not retain to 40 YOS at these rates, more O-5s would be promoted to O-6 and more O-4s to O-5. If the community fails to retain even close to these predictions, the accessions will decrease less than we have posited and promotion rates will increase. Regardless, average experience will likely increase and accessions will decrease if behavior moves in this direction. In fact, as posited here, the average experience of officers would be 16.5, 23.5, and 29.3 YOS for O-4s, O-5s, and O-6s, respectively.

This program is by far the broadest application of an alternative to up-or-out for any of the communities or services discussed in this report. As such, it could have a greater impact on accessions and promotions than the other programs. That is why we proposed some relief from the prescribed grade pyramid for O-4s and O-5s. Another consequence is that the FAO community must receive 100 percent of its targeted designations. Given that the number of O-4s entering the community could decrease to less than 50 officers per year, any missed designations could result in a greater proportion of total designations. Additionally, with officers serving longer as FAOs, each unfilled designation requirement results in more lost man-years over the course of a career.

One of the disadvantages of such a revised system with greater tenure and experience is the loss of some flexibility. For example, should there be a dramatic change in the foreign area expertise needed by the Army, the FAO community could have a difficult time responding because of the reduced designations and longer tenure of officers with the previously prioritized area specialties. One solution would be to cross train officers in different world areas in order to preserve some system

---

[12] Should the retirement system be revised so that field-grade officers continue to increase their retirement by 2.5 percent each year past 30 YOS, the continuation rate at 30 YOS might change so more officers continue past 30 YOS. Given the relatively small number of officers that we modeled as remaining in the community at 30 YOS, this would have only an incremental effect on promotion or community accessions.

flexibility. This would avoid the predicament of having a disproportionate number of FAOs trained in a no-longer-hot geographic region. However, an officer trained in Arabic and Portuguese would likely not prove as mission valuable as one trained in geographically similar areas and languages, such as Arabic and Farsi.

Reduced designations also have another implication for the training pipeline. The reduced throughput means that some regional and language training may be sporadic; some languages and regional expertise may not be taught with every cohort group.

Demonstration Design and Evaluation. The demonstration proposed above for Army FAOs will be conducted as a quasi-experiment. The demonstration group will consist of all Army FAOs, and likely comparison groups will be FAOs in other services, previous cohorts of Army FAOs, and perhaps members of the Army Acquisition Corps—the other functional area in the Operational Support career field. The large numbers of participants make detection of significant effects much more likely than in the other three demonstrations proposed in this report. However, the lack of random assignment of participants to groups will make ruling out alternative explanations of the results difficult in some cases.

The program for FAOs is not simply aimed at addressing manning shortages but rather fundamentally changing the way officer careers are managed, and the evaluation plan should reflect that purpose. Program monitoring in this case will be relatively straightforward. The most important implementation detail to monitor will be the reasons for separation. Interviews and document review can be used to verify that officers twice failed for promotion are no longer automatically separated and that employability determines continued service after 20 YOS. Any planned changes to training incentives or requirements should also be monitored.

A broad set of measures will be required to adequately assess all the outcomes of interest. Promotion rates (both in-zone and above-zone), retention rates, and new FAO accessions at O-3 and designations at O-4 should be monitored for the demonstration and comparison groups. Data on numbers and proficiency levels of FAOs qualified in two AOCs will be of interest, as will average career length. Those objective data can be complemented by information on the perceptions and satisfaction not only of officers in the program but of the agencies or commands that employ them.

For a program of the size proposed, cost becomes an important consideration. Data on program costs should be considered in the context of changes in effectiveness. In this case, effectiveness could be measured through tests of proficiency of individual officers or with appropriate measures of FAO mission fulfillment.

Policy Package 3: The SWO Specialist Program

The Navy is short hundreds of SWOs at the grades of O-4 and O-5 due to missed accession goals and historically low retention rates in the 1990s. The shortages are expected to continue for at least several years to come. To help ameliorate the shortages, the Navy pays SWOs bonuses totaling $50,000 to complete their department head tours and up to $46,000 for SWOs who elect to stay to three years beyond department head as O-4s. We designed a policy package to explore nonpecuniary incentives that could lead to greater retention and fewer shortages of SWOs at the grade of O-4.

One obstacle to retention is the fact that O-4s who do not screen successfully for executive officer (XO) stand little chance for promotion to O-5. SWOs get up to three "looks" for XO after promotion to O-4, typically in their tenth, eleventh, and twelfth YOS. At about their thirteenth year those who are selected begin their XO tour, which is a prerequisite for promotion to O-5. With the up-or-out law, officers not promoted to O-5 will have to leave active duty unless they are within two years of retirement or a board selects them for continuation. While SELCON could allow them to serve up to 24 years on active duty, their last pay increase as an O-4 would come at the eighteenth year. Furthermore, they would spend much of their remaining time labeled as failures of selection for promotion, and they and their families might continue to be moved every few years with a new assignment. Once officers do not screen for XO and are therefore unlikely to be promoted to O-5, many transfer to another community or leave the service altogether.

One could argue that the very best officers are selected for XO, but it is widely recognized that with a surface warfare community of more than 8,000 officers and only 240 surface ships to serve in as XO and commanding officer, competition is fierce and many capable officers are not selected. Many junior SWOs, in fact, do not even aspire to command at sea, according to junior officer surveys sponsored by the SWO community.[13] Yet they must serve in those positions if they wish to remain in the Navy, thereby filling billets that might have gone to other officers who do wish to command.

Program Overview

We have designed a policy package that will enable 10 to 15 O-4s per year who do not screen for XO to serve in certain shore-based billets as "SWO specialists" (or a similar job title), with incentives and opportunities to serve up to 24 YOS. The goals of this SWO Specialist Program are to address the Navy's need to retain more midgrade officers with sea duty experience and to provide an attractive career alternative for SWOs not selected for XO afloat that do not follow the command-and-promote path. Once in these alternative paths, officers who are not selected for promotion would continue without requiring consideration by SELCON boards.

Criteria for Participation. Selection will occur at one of two points in an officer's career. Most officers will be selected after their cohort's third screen for XO, around the twelfth YOS. They will remain in the grade of O-4 and will serve as SWO specialists from approximately the fourteenth YOS through the twentieth. At that point they will be subject to a formal review and could be given the opportunity to continue to 24 years. A smaller number of O-4s will be selected as new participants at their twentieth YOS, when they become retirement eligible. They, too, will be given the opportunity to continue to 24 YOS. Once the program is mature, a single SWO specialist board (with membership typical for such boards) can handle all selection and continuation decisions. It will select officers at the two career points

---

[13]   Surface Warfare Officer Junior Officer Survey, 1999 and 2001.

and also selectively continue officers already in the program as they reach their twentieth YOS.

Program Size. Although we do not prescribe a specific number of officers to be selected for this program, we envision a fairly small program: about ten selected at the first point and five selected at the second. If ten officers were chosen every year after their third XO screen, they would fill no more than 100 SWO specialist billets at any given time (ten officers in each of ten cohorts up through 24 YOS). If another five officers were selected as they approached retirement and served from year 21 until year 24, they would fill an additional 20 billets.

Assignments. The officers chosen for the program after the third XO screen will complete their current assignments and will receive their first SWO specialist assignment around their fourteenth YOS. This is also the point at which many O-4s today leave. The officers will be given a six-year, shore-based assignment (with the guarantee of geographical stability), where they will serve as recognized experts in their fields. Engineers, for example, could perform their duties at Readiness Support or Afloat Training Groups at Fleet concentration areas where they would train ships' engineering departments as they begin workups for deployments.

Incentives and Compensation. One of the key incentives in this program is the guarantee of geographical stability for officers who probably will not be promoted beyond O-4. These officers will be in their mid- to late-30s and many will have families, making permanent changes of station an increasingly negative quality-of-life issue. The first assignment would provide at least six years for a shore assignment (in the same geographical location). An officer's tenure could be extended an additional four years (after the review board) beyond the twentieth YOS, where the officer could be given a new, four-year assignment.

An incentive may be necessary to entice SWO O-4s beyond their twentieth YOS. The last longevity basic pay increase for an O-4 occurs at the eighteenth YOS, after which basic pay rises only through yearly cost-of-living increases. Retention bonuses can be used to compensate SWO specialists who remain beyond their twentieth YOS. The bonuses would not have to be large to be on par with basic pay raises for O-5s as they reach 22 and 24 YOS.[14]

CSRB authority and TSP contributions can provide additional compensation to participating officers, and, as noted earlier, the SWO specialists will remain eligible for promotion. Those who are promoted to O-5 can continue to 28 YOS and can even be considered for further promotion and longer service. Most officers in this program, however, will likely retire as O-4s. Those that do could receive a tombstone promotion to O-5. However, those that make O-5 while on active duty will not receive a tombstone promotion to O-6.

Training. Program participants typically will have obtained a master's degree earlier in their careers, so an extended period for schooling will not be needed. To keep current in their fields, officers will have shorter periods of education and training, perhaps 90 to 120 days, every two to three years.

Impact on Community. With any of these programs, if some officers have longer careers as a result of the new policies, the community or service may wish to lower accessions to save on training costs. This will not happen as soon as the policies are implemented because it will be too early to tell how career patterns change. Nevertheless, we can use models to estimate how the program would affect end strength at maturity. The modeling methodology is outlined in Appendix E.

The program impact is measured in terms of total man-years served by a cohort through the course of a 30-year career, and we translate this into possible accession decreases. Our low estimate is a negligible change in man-years, assuming that participants would have served 24-year careers anyway. Our high estimate is an increase of 120 man-years, assuming that all participants would have left the surface warfare community immediately upon nonselection for XO or upon reaching 20 YOS (depending on when they are selected to participate). The middle-ground estimate is an increase of 74.8 man-

---

[14] Currently O-5s receive a 2.7 percent pay raise after 20 years and another 3.0 percent raise after 22 years. Using the January 2003 pay tables, those equate to about an $1,800 increase for O-4s at year 20 and a $2,000 increase at year 22.

years, assuming that participants would have continuation patterns similar to the entire cohort.[15]

The middle and high estimates would enable accessions to decrease by about 1 percent to 2 percent, which is basically a margin of error for accession goals. This leads to two preliminary observations: First, a small program such as this in a community as large as surface warfare will have very small systemic effects. Second, to the extent that the SWO Specialist Program is intended to have a real impact on the inventory-authorization imbalance (not only does the surface warfare community have a shortage of O-4s and O-5s but it also has an excess of O-1s and O-2s), it will have to be larger than we have proposed as a demonstration project.

Demonstration Design and Evaluation. Due to the small numbers of officers expected to participate in the proposed program, it is highly unlikely that an experimental or quasi-experimental design could yield statistically detectable effects. This program should thus be conducted as a qualitative case study, and interpreters of the outcomes should refrain from assuming results will be generalizable either to other officers in the SWO community or to other officer communities. Nevertheless, a number of outcomes can be measured with respect to the SWO specialists, some of which are discussed below.

The program proposed above aims to satisfy a straightforward goal, namely to address current shortages of O-4s in the surface warfare community by enhancing retention rather than increasing accessions. The most basic measure of the program's success in reaching that goal is the change in the number of O-4s as a result of the demonstration. Changes in several factors other than the proposed intervention can affect the number of O-4s at different points in time, including the following:

- promotion rates, most immediately from O-3 to O-4 and from O-4 to O-5
- accessions (in the longer term)
- number of O-4s accepting traditional offers for SELCON
- number of O-4s within two years of retirement
- lateral entry from or exit to other communities or services.

---

[15] See Appendix E for detailed calculations.

Efforts should therefore be made to determine whether any of these other factors might be causing observed changes in the number of O-4s.

Another outcome of interest would be changes in the number of O-5s as a result of the introduction of the SWO specialist track. As indicated above, there is some chance that O-4 specialists would still be promoted to O-5. It is also conceivable that the introduction of the demonstration could have a negative effect on the output of the regular promotion system. For instance, if significant numbers of SWOs perceive the SWO specialist path as preferable to promotion to O-5 (due to more stable assignments, for instance), more junior SWOs or identifiable subsets of them might pursue experiences that are less likely to lead them to promotion. The same sorts of factors that must be considered in interpreting changes in the numbers of O-4s should be considered when analyzing any changes in the numbers of O-5s.

A group of measures could also be targeted at assessing the attractiveness of the SWO specialist option. Information on the number of O-4s who are offered the alternative career path and their take rate can be compared with data on the career paths of O-4s in previous cohorts who did not screen for XO. How many left active duty? How many were offered SELCON? How many accepted? How long did they stay? Those quantitative measures can be complemented by qualitative measures aimed at discovering officers' reasons for accepting or rejecting offers to be SWO specialists at 14 and 20 YOS, as well as data on the satisfaction of those who choose the SWO specialist option.

Policy Package 4: Marine Corps Retention of Highly Valued Officers

Each policy package presented in this document has unique aspects, yet there are similarities between them as well. The Marine policy package is unique because it will be implemented servicewide but will be similar in size and selectivity to that of the Navy. It will make continuation subject to decentralized decisions about an officer's performance-based employability in a specific assignment, similar to the Air Force and FAO policy packages. The Marine policy package also aims to explore how officer careers could be managed differently, rather than trying to address any manning shortages. In that regard it is more like the Army FAO policy package.

Program Overview

This policy package will allow the Marine Corps to retain a small number of O-4s, O-5s, and O-6s to fill headquarters staff jobs where longer tenure and greater experience will improve organizational effectiveness. Individual officers will be nominated by a command or agency to fill a specific billet, subject to approval by a senior officer. The goal is to give the Marine Corps greater flexibility in the career management and retention of highly valued field-grade officers.

Criteria for Participation. Eligible candidates are field-grade officers who would otherwise require SELCON to remain on active duty. The pool of candidates includes O-4s who are twice failed of selection for promotion and O-5s and O-6s who have reached 28 and 30 years of active commissioned service, respectively. An officer must be nominated for a specific assignment within a command or headquarters, and all nominees will be subject to approval by a senior officer. This approval could be in the form of making the actual selection or approving the results of a nonstatutory selection board. (A waiver to Title 10 to allow this in lieu of the normal working of a SELCON board would be needed.) Approved officers will be offered a contract to serve within the position for a period of three to five years. Participating O-4s may remain on active duty until 24 YOS, O-5s may remain until 32 YOS, and O-6s until 34 YOS.

Program Size. The program could be designed around a fixed number of assignments, with nominations based on vacancies, or it could be designed so that a prescribed number of officers are nominated each year. Either way, the Marines we spoke with expressed their desire to keep the program small, accepting approximately five O-4s, two O-5s, and two O-6s per year. If the average assignment length is four years and nine officers are selected to participate annually, there would be about 36 billets filled once the program is mature.

Assignments. As with the Air Force Effective Manning Fill, officers will be required to have the appropriate military occupational specialty (MOS) and grade for the billet, but specific assignments will be determined by the contracts with the command or headquarters.

Because the program is not restricted to specific occupations, the billets filled and officers accepted may change according to the needs of the corps. However, there will be significant continuity for the individual officers, whose assignments will last from three to five years.

Incentives and Compensation. As with the other policy packages Marines will receive retention bonuses commensurate with a longevity basic pay increase. They will enjoy greater geographical stability with longer assignments late in their careers and will continue to be eligible for promotion while on active duty.

Training. One key benefit for both the officers and the Marine Corps is greater visibility to a career of 24 years for O-4s, 32 years for O-5s, and 34 years for O-6s. Officers may be identified as candidates before they actually reach the point where they are nominated for the program and can be groomed for long-serving jobs at the end of their careers by means of training or an earlier assignment.

At the time of nomination officers must be qualified to fill the specific billet in which they will serve. They will be expected to keep current on skills needed for their assignments, but additional training will probably not be necessary once an officer has filled a billet.

Impact on Community. This program is intended not to address retention or accession issues but to change the way officer careers are managed. Therefore, no significant effect on manpower is expected. The program will, however, streamline the process of retaining specific individuals and will remove some of the uncertainty for both the officers and the Marines.

Demonstration Design and Evaluation. The program proposed here for the Marine Corps clearly lends itself best to a qualitative case study design. The numbers of participants will be purposely kept small; participants will be handpicked, not selected randomly; and there is no need to generalize results to a large population. In this case, qualitative measures targeted at the outcomes of interest will be of particular importance. Because the numbers of officers in the program will be small, in-depth interviews at selected times and using a formal interview protocol can be conducted with program participants and officers up the chain of command. Information can be collected about each feature of the program, including assignments, training, and compensation to make local adjustments that calibrate the program to current and anticipated Marine Corps needs.

Table 5.1
Summary of Demonstration Project Proposals

	Air Force	Army FAOs	Navy SWOs	Marines
Project goal	To provide high-performing officers with a clear view of long military careers outside of the command-and-promote path. Projects will test alternatives to current policies, identify challenges in implementation, and measure individual and organizational satisfaction with outcomes			
Eligible officers	O4s, O5s in shortage AFSC not selected for in-residence PME	Entire community (O4s through O6s)	O4s not screened for XO after cohort's third XO screen	O4s, O5s, and O6s in any occupation
Approximate program size	25 O4s, 20 O5s per year; 480 O4s, 250 O5s total	Current community size is 1,000	15 per year; 120 total	9 per year; 36 total
Criteria to participate	Random selection may be feasible	Field-area designation as FAO	Board-screened for initial entry; review at 20 YOS	Nomination by command or agency; approval by Commandant
	Continuation will be contingent upon having a renewable employment commitment from an agency or command			
Assignments	Depend on needs of community/service and interest of officers but are expected to be longer than typical today			
Compensation	Existing statutes allowing for incentive bonuses, Thrift Savings Plan contributions, and tombstone promotions to compensate officers serving longer careers			
Other incentives	Officers continue to be eligible for promotion while on active duty. Longer assignments give officers and their families increased geographical stability. Commands and agencies have incentive to participate due to increased personnel continuity, organizational stability			
Maximum career length	O4s: 30 YOS O5s: 30 YOS	O4s: 40 YOS O5s: 40 YOS O6s: 40 YOS	O4s: 24 YOS	O4s: 24 YOS O5s: 32 YOS O6s: 34 YOS
Type of demonstration	Experiment	Quasi-experiment	Case study	Case study
Comparison groups	Eligible officers not randomly selected	Other services' FAOs; prior FAO cohorts; other Army communities	N/A	N/A
Applicability	Individuals in multiple communities	Community	Individuals within community	Individuals within service

CHAPTER SIX

Next Steps

If alternatives to the up-or-stay system are to be implemented as demonstration projects, two things must first happen: The services and OSD must formally agree to put such a project and its constituent policies in place, and Congress must grant the authority to do so. OSD bears the responsibility for seeing that both occur. We have recommended that OSD seek demonstration project authority for military personnel similar to that granted to the Executive Branch for civilian personnel in Title 5 of the United States Code. We have also met with representatives of each of the services several times and have designed four specific policy packages with input from the services and communities affected. These recommendations to the project sponsors are not intended to foreclose the opportunity to develop additional policy packages for other communities or to modify the existing packages. Indeed, some negotiation or further discussion is expected between OSD and the services to put actual programs in place. The aim of the project is to begin implementation of the policies in FY 2005.

The other set of recommendations we have presented here relates to evaluation of the processes by which the policies are implemented and of their outcomes for both individuals and communities. Evaluation will be based on an assortment of qualitative and quantitative data and will be conducted as the demonstration projects are ongoing. NDRI will continue to play a consultative role to support the analysis and refinement of the projects and will specify implementation and evaluation plans in more detail as decisions are made about whether and how these specific demonstration projects will proceed.

The length of the implementation phase is indeterminate. As originally envisioned this project was to last a minimum of four years, with the middle two years allocated to conducting the demonstration projects themselves. However, the demonstration projects may require more than two years to generate meaningful results, and if they are implemented broadly for a large number of officers, the demonstration projects may simply become de facto new policy. This would not be unprecedented. Demonstration projects implemented for civilian personnel have, in some cases, continued for many years.

NDRI will analyze the progress and results of the demonstration projects and will develop findings and recommendations for OSD. These may be presented while the demonstration projects are still running. Evaluation will include analyzing expected resulting grade structures, career tenure profiles, accession requirements, and costs or savings generated. We will offer, where applicable, recommendations regarding program design features, such as structuring of incentives, the officers to include in such programs, and other refinements that would likely lead to greater cost savings, a higher response rate, or other desirable outcomes. NDRI will recommend exit strategies as necessary when OSD wishes to terminate a demonstration project. Finally, the evaluations will address the advisability of administering the tested policies more broadly or making them permanent.

DoD Civilian Workforce Demonstration Projects

Table A.1
PACER SHARE Productivity and Personnel Management Demonstration Baseline Evaluation and Third-Year Evaluation

Occupations	Civilians working in Air Logistics
Duration	5 years; 1988–1993
Description	PACER SHARE was a five-year productivity and personnel management demonstration project initiated by the Directorate of Distribution at the Sacramento Air Logistics Center (ALC) under the authority of Title VI of the Civil Service Reform Act to determine whether experimental changes would improve organizational productivity, flexibility, and quality of work life while sustaining the quality and timeliness of work and the capability of mobilizing during emergencies or wartime.
Experiment and analysis	RAND worked with the Directorates of Distribution, Personnel, and Accounting and Finance at McClellan Air Force Base and with OPM to design five interventions: • job series consolidation • revised base pay determination • revised supervisory grading criteria • revised hiring and retention criteria • productivity gain sharing. Impact Analysis. Four other ALCs that perform similar functions as the Sacramento ALC test site collectively served as the comparison group before and during the project. The authors state, "differences among the ALCs at the outset of the demonstration are netted out by comparing outcomes at Sacramento and the comparison group to their own baselines. Effects of systemwide changes should be picked up in trends at the comparison group. Subtracting the latter from the trend at the demonstration site should then yield evidence of the demonstration's effects."[a]

Measurement Approach [b]				
Area of Analysis	Instrument/Method	Data Collector	Schedule	Source
Changes in productivity	Cost savings analysis	Directorate of Accounting and Finance; Directorate of Distribution (DS)	Baseline, monthly during demo	Existing databases; Sacramento and comparison sites

Organizational flexibility and quality of work life	Attitude survey	RAND	Baseline, annually during demo	DS employees; Sacramento and comparison sites
	Personnel Office Productivity Analysis (POPA)	Directorate of Personnel (DP), OPM	Baseline, quarterly during demo	All DP employees servicing DS; Sacramento and comparison sites
	Personnel records	DP, OPM	Baseline, annually during demo	Manual record systems; Sacramento and comparison sites
	Workforce database	DP, OPM	Baseline, annually during demo	Existing personnel records; Sacramento and comparison sites
Quality and timeliness of work in DS	Quality/timeliness analysis	Quality and management divisions in DS	Baseline, monthly or quarterly during demo	Existing data on work quality, timeliness; authorized audits undertaken by DS; Sacramento and comparison sites

Outcomes   The results of the evaluation included the following:

- organizational flexibility was increased but not in every area of the organization
- strong evidence of increased quality of work life under PACER SHARE
- work timeliness and quality measures showed an overall deterioration (but may have been attributable to other events)
- cost-effectiveness was not increased under the PACER SHARE program

It is unclear what the exit strategy was for this evaluation, but the report implies that it remained in place after the evaluation was complete

a Orvis, Hosek, and Mattock, 1993, p. 19.
b A useful overview of the evaluation model can be found in Orvis, Hosek, and Mattock, 1993, Table 3 on pp. 15–18.
SOURCE: Bruce R. Orvis, James R. Hosek, and Michael G. Mattock, *Productivity and Personnel Management Demonstration Baseline Evaluation*, Santa Monica, Calif.: RAND Corporation, R-3753-FMP, 1990; and Bruce R. Orvis, James R. Hosek, and Michael G. Mattock, *PACER SHARE: Productivity and Personnel Management Demonstration, Third Year Evaluation*, Santa Monica, Calif.: RAND Corporation, MR-310-P&R, 1993.

Table A.2
Naval Sea Systems Command Warfare Centers Demonstration Project

Occupations	Virtually all of the more than 20,000 civilian employees of both the Naval Surface Warfare Center and the Naval Undersea Warfare Center. The warfare centers are comprised of a total of seven divisions with many major sites nationwide.
Duration	5 years; Naval Surface Warfare Center: 1998 to present; Naval Undersea Warfare Center: 1999 to present
Description	The goal of the demonstration project is to implement a human resource management system that successfully attracts, develops, and retains high-performing employees. Specific objectives are to provide
	• a simplified human resource management system that is understandable to employees
	• continued development for all employees
	• incentives for performance contributions
	• flexibility to meet the needs of the organization in changing environments
	• delegated decisionmaking to lower levels in the organization
	• avenues for union and management collaborative problem solving and decisionmaking
	• fairness, acceptability, and humaneness
	• cost controllability.
	There are five major components of the project: (1) broad banding classification system; (2) performance development system; (3) incentive pay system; (4) RIF system; and (5) competitive examining and scholastic appointments (hiring).
	While the personnel demonstration project and its five components cover all General Schedule (GS) employees, the Federal Wage System employees are included only for purposes of changes in the performance development, RIF, and competitive examining systems. Likewise, Senior-Level and Scientific and Technical employees are covered only under the incentive pay, performance development, and RIF systems. Basic elements of the five components are applied uniformly throughout the Divisions through policies established at the warfare center level.[a]
Measurement approach	"Information from existing management systems, supplemented with perceptual data gathered from employee attitude surveys, focus group discussions, and interviews will be used to measure the success of the Project."[b]

[a] Naval Sea Systems Command Warfare Centers Demonstration Project Web site, http://www.nswc.navy.mil/P/DEMO/ (as of June 3, 2003).
[b] Naval Sea Systems, 2003.

Table A.3
Naval Personnel Demonstration Project ("China Lake")

Occupations	10,000 scientists and engineers, technicians, administrative, technical specialists, and clerical staff
Duration	1980–1994; made permanent
Description	The China Lake project was the first personnel demonstration project under Title VI of the Civil Service Reform Act. The labs were interested in improving recruitment and retention of high-quality workers and increasing management flexibility by increasing their control over classification, pay, and other personnel matters. Classification was simplified and delegated to managers. Pay increases with broad pay bands were linked closely to performance ratings, and starting salaries were made flexible.[a]
Experiment and analysis	The demonstration project involved four labs; it was implemented at two naval research and development laboratories: the Naval Ocean Systems Center and the Naval Weapons Center served as test sites and the Naval Air Development Center and the Naval Surface Weapons Center served as the control sites.
Measurement approach	Data were collected from several sources:

- annual attitude surveys: administered to all supervisors and a 25% stratified random sample of all demonstration equivalent employees at the four labs
- standardized on-site interviews with scientists, engineers, and technicians, called "personnel management assessment modules": assess classification accuracy, adequacy, and timeliness; performance planning and appraisal procedures; level of authority for personnel decisionmaking and adherence to merit system principles
- workforce data
- various documents provided by the four test labs.

Outcomes	OPM conducted the project evaluation and concluded that the demonstration program "was successful in improving personnel management at the two demonstrations labs. Simplified delegated job classification...has drastically reduced the time for classification actions and reduced conflict between personnel and managers. Average salaries have increased two to three percent under the pay banding. Recruitment, retention and reduced turnover of high performers and increased turnover of low performers have all improved. Perceived supervisory authority over classification, pay and hiring increased, as did employee satisfaction with pay and performance management; more than 70 percent of employees are supporting the demonstration system."[b]

[a]See www.opm.gov/demos/.
[b]See www.opm.gov/demos/.

Table A.4
U.S. Naval Research Laboratory Personnel Management Demonstration Project

Occupations	All Navy Research Laboratory (NRL) employees except Senior Executive Service (SES) Scientific and Technical employees, guards, and trade and craft employees
Duration	1999 to present
Description	The project was established under the National Defense Authorization Act for FY 1995, which authorized the establishment of Science and Technology (S&T) Reinvention Laboratories in DoD. "The purpose of the NRL project is to . . . enhance the Laboratory's ability to attract, retain, and motivate a high-quality workforce. To this end, the project involves: 1) streamlined hiring processes; 2) broad banding; 3) simplified position classification; 4) a contribution-based compensation system; 5) extended probationary period for new employees and 6) modified reduction in force procedures."[a]
Experiment and analysis	"A modified quasi-experimental design will be used for the evaluation of the S&T Laboratory Demonstration Program. Because most of the eligible labs are participating in the program . . . comparison group will be compiled from the Civilian Personnel Data File. This comparison group will consist of workforce data from Government-wide research organizations in civilian Federal agencies with missions and job series matching those in the DoD laboratories . . . the original China Lake project will serve as a second comparison group which can be used as a benchmark representing a stable broad banding system. The two original Navy demonstration labs will participate in the employee survey and will also provide workforce data . . . staggered implementation of the demonstration program across labs will also allow for time series analyses using multiple baselines."[b]
Measurement approach	Both quantitative and qualitative data will be collected: • workforce data • personnel office and other data on quality and timeliness • employee attitude surveys • survey of human resources orientation • research ratings for scientists and engineers to be used in turnover analysis • structured interviews and focus group data • local site historian logs and implementation information.

[a]U.S. Naval Research Laboratory (NRL) Personnel Management Demonstration Project; Department of the Navy (DON), Washington D.C.; Notice, *Federal Register*, Vol. 64, No. 121, June 24, 1999, p. 33970.
[b]U.S. Naval Research Laboratory, 1999, p. 34007.

Table A.5
Laboratory Personnel Management Demonstration Project at Department of the Air Force Research Labs

Occupations	Initially only scientists and engineers were included in the project.
Duration	1996 to present
Description	"The project was designed by the Department of the Air Force with participation of and review by the DoD and the OPM. The purpose of the project is to achieve the best workforce for the laboratory mission, adjust the workforce for change and improve workforce quality. The project framework addresses all aspects of the human resource life cycle model. There are three major areas of change: a) laboratory-controlled rapid hiring; b) a contribution-based compensation system and c) a streamlined removal process."[a]
Experiment and analysis	"The external evaluation for the four Air Force Labs is part of a larger effort involving evaluation of demonstration projects in a total of 24 reinvention labs in three military services. . . . Overseen by the Office of Merit Systems Oversight and Effectiveness, OPM, and the Director Defense Research and Engineering and Civilian Personnel Policy. OPM's Personnel Resources and Development Center will serve in the role of the external evaluator. . . . A quasi-experimental design with pre- and post-implementation comparisons will be employed. Baseline measures are being taken prior to project implementation. Then, repeated measurements will be taken post-implementation to allow longitudinal comparisons by intervention within and across the four AF labs. Additional features of the design call for comparisons of AF results to those for the other 20 service labs that are expected to be part of the demonstration program, as well as to those for the original Navy demonstration project conducted at China Lake and San Diego. Further comparisons for pay purposes will be conducted with a composite comparison group covering similar occupations and job series to be constructed from OPM's Central Personnel Data File."[b] **Exit Strategy.** "In the event the project ends, a conversion back to the former (regular) Federal civil service system will be required. All employees in a broadband level corresponding to a single GS grade will be converted to that grade. Employees in a multiple grade broadband level will be considered to have attained the next higher grade when they have been in the level at least one year . . . employees who leave the demonstration project and return to the GS pay system via reassignment, promotion, demotion or transfer are subject to parallel pay conversion rules to determine the converted GS rates."[c]

Table A.5—(continued)

Measurement approach	An attitude survey, structured interviews, and focus groups will be conducted to measure perceived organizational flexibility and perceived time savings from reduced administrative workload, employee perceptions of advancement, pay satisfaction, internal and external equity, perceived motivational power, fairness of awards, pay-contribution link, fairness of ratings, trust in supervisors, and adequacy of performance feedback.
	Workforce data will be collected on starting salaries of banded versus nonbanded employees; progression of new hires over time by band, career path; mean salaries by band, career path, demographics; total payroll cost; number of employees at high grade salaries pre- and post-banding; amount and number of awards by career path, pay-contribution correlations, turnover by contribution assessment.

[a]Laboratory Personnel Management Demonstration Project; Department of the Air Force; Notice, *Federal Register*, Vol. 61, No. 230, November 27, 1996, p. 60403.
[b]Laboratory Personnel Management, 1996, p. 60421–60422.
[c]Laboratory Personnel Management, 1996, p. 60421.

Table A.6
Science and Technology Reinvention Laboratory Demonstration Project at the Army Research Laboratory

Occupations	All GS employees except SES, employees classified in the Scientific and Professional pay plan, Federal Wage System employees (to be included later), and Civilian Intelligence Personnel Management System employees
Duration	1998 to present
Description	The project was established under the National Defense Authorization Act of FY 1995, which authorized the establishment of S&T Reinvention Laboratories in DoD. Designed by the Army Research Lab, the project is intended to provide managers with greater flexibility and control in order to improve the hiring, retention, and performance of its employees. The project includes the following components: broad banding, a pay-for-performance system, a new classification system, new hiring and appointment authorities, expanded employee development programs, and revised RIF procedures.
Experiment and analysis	"An evaluation plan for the entire laboratory demonstration program covering 24 DoD labs was developed by a joint OPM/DoD Evaluation Committee . . . and will be coordinated and conducted by OPM's Personnel Resources and Development . . . An intervention impact model will be used to measure the effectiveness of the various personnel system changes or interventions . . . the main focus of the evaluation will be on the intermediate outcomes, i.e., the results specific personnel system changes which are expected to improve human resources management. The ultimate outcomes are defined as improved organizational effectiveness, mission accomplishment, and customer satisfaction."[a]
	Exit strategy: See *Federal Register* for detailed conversion procedures.
Measurement approach	An attitude survey, structured interviews, and focus groups will be conducted to measure organizational flexibility and time savings from reduced administrative workload, pay satisfaction, internal and external equity, perceived motivational power, fairness of awards, pay-contribution link, fairness of ratings, trust in supervisors, and adequacy of performance feedback.
	Workforce data will be collected on starting salaries of banded versus nonbanded employees; progression of new hires over time by band, career path; mean salaries by band, career path, demographics; total payroll cost; number of employees at high grade salaries pre- and post-banding; amount and number of awards by career path, pay-contribution correlations, turnover by contribution assessment.

[a]Science and Technology Reinvention Laboratory Personnel Demonstration Project at the U.S. Army Research Laboratory (ARL); Notice, *Federal Register*, Vol. 63, No. 42, March 4, 1998, p. 10698.

Table A.7
Science and Technology Reinvention Laboratory Personnel Demonstration Project at the Army Aviation Research, Development, and Engineering Center

Occupations	Civilian appropriate funded employees in the competitive and excepted service paid under the GS system. Scientific and Professional employees and positions will be included for employee development, performance appraisal and award provisions only; their classification, staffing, and compensation will not change. SES, Federal Wage System employees, Department of the Army (DA) interns and employees in the quality assurance specialist career program will not be covered.
Duration	1997 to present
Description	The project was established under the National Defense Authorization Act of FY 1995, which authorized the establishment of S&T Reinvention Laboratories in DoD. Designed by the DA, the project is intended to provide managers with greater flexibility and control in order to improve the hiring, retention, and performance of its employees. The project includes the following components: broad banding, a pay-for-performance system, a new classification system, new hiring and appointment authorities, expanded employee development programs, and revised RIF procedures.
Experiment and analysis	OPM's Personnel Resources and Development Center will conduct the evaluation. "An intervention impact model will be used to measure the effectiveness of the various personnel system changes or interventions . . . the main focus of the evaluation will be on the intermediate outcomes, i.e., the results specific personnel system changes which are expected to improve human resources management. The ultimate outcomes are defined as improved organizational effectiveness, mission accomplishment, and customer satisfaction."[a]
	Exit Strategy: See *Federal Register* for detailed conversion procedures.
Measurement approach	An attitude survey, structured interviews, and focus groups will be conducted to measure perceived organizational flexibility and perceived time savings from reduced administrative workload, employee perceptions of advancement, pay satisfaction, internal and external equity, perceived motivational power, fairness of awards, pay-contribution link, fairness of ratings, trust in supervisors, and adequacy of performance feedback.
	Workforce data will be collected on starting salaries of banded versus nonbanded employees; progression of new hires over time by band, career path; mean salaries by band, career path, demographics; total payroll cost; number of employees at high grade salaries pre- and post-banding; amount and number of awards by career path, pay-contribution correlations, turnover by contribution assessment.

[a]Science and Technology Reinvention Laboratory Personnel Demonstration Project at the Aviation Research, Development, and Engineering Center; Notice, *Federal Register*, Vol. 62, No. 124, June 27, 1997, p. 34923.

Table A.8
Science and Technology Laboratory Personnel Management Demonstration Project at the Army Engineer Waterways Experiment Station

Occupations	All GS employees employed by the center; does not include Civilian Intelligence Personnel Management System employees or Scientific and Technical employees
Duration	1997 to present
Description	Established under the National Defense Authorization Act of FY 1995, which authorized the establishment of S&T Reinvention Laboratories in DoD. "Designed by the Assistant Secretary of the Army for Research, Development and Acquisition, with the support of the Assistant Secretary of the Army for Civil Works and the participation of the five Army S&T Reinvention Labs . . . this project is built upon the concepts of linking performance to pay for all covered positions, simplifying paperwork in the processing of classification and other personnel actions, emphasizing partnerships among management, employees and unions, and delegating other authorities to line managers."[a]
Experiment and analysis	The evaluation will be conducted by OPM's Personnel Resources and Development Center . . . selected parts of the evaluation will be completed using contractor support. . . . "An intervention impact model will be used to measure the effectiveness of the various personnel system changes or interventions . . . the main focus of the evaluation will be on the intermediate outcomes, i.e., the results specific personnel system changes which are expected to improve human resources management." The ultimate outcomes are defined as improved organizational effectiveness, mission accomplishment, and customer satisfaction.
Measurement approach	An attitude survey, structured interviews, and focus groups will be conducted to measure perceived organizational flexibility and perceived time savings from reduced administrative workload, employee perceptions of advancement, pay satisfaction, internal and external equity, perceived motivational power, fairness of awards, pay-contribution link, fairness of ratings, trust in supervisors, and adequacy of performance feedback.
	Workforce data will be collected on starting salaries of banded versus nonbanded employees; progression of new hires over time by band, career path; mean salaries by band, career path, demographics; total payroll cost; number of employees at high grade salaries pre- and post-banding; amount and number of awards by career path, pay-contribution correlations, turnover by contribution assessment.

[a]Science and Technology Reinvention Laboratory Personnel Demonstration Project Final Plan: U.S. Army Engineer Waterways Experiment Station (WES), Vicksburg, Miss.; Notice; Republication, *Federal Register*, Vol. 63, No. 57, March 25, 1998, p. 14583.

Table A.9
Laboratory Personnel Management Demonstration Project at the Army Medical Research and Materiel Command

Occupations	GS employees and DA interns. It does not include SES employees, Scientific and Professional employees, Federal Wage System employees, and those in the GS-080 series covered by the Civilian Intelligence Personnel Management System.
Duration	1998 to present
Description	Established under the National Defense Authorization Act of FY 1995, which authorized the establishment of S&T Reinvention Laboratories in DoD. Designed by the Department of the Army "the purpose of this project is to demonstrate that the effectiveness of [DoD labs] can be enhanced by allowing greater managerial control over personnel functions and, at the same time, expanding the opportunities available to employees through a more responsive and flexible personnel system . . . [expected outcomes include:] (a) Increased quality in the total workforce and the products they produce; (b) increased timeliness of key personnel processes; (c) increased retention of high quality employees and increased non-retention of poor quality employees; and (d) increased satisfaction with MRMC and its products by all customers it serves."[a] The project will introduce broad banding, a new classification system, a pay-for-performance management system, hiring and appointment authorities, expanded developmental opportunities for employees, and revised RIF procedures.
Experiment and analysis	"The evaluation will focus on the continuum of personnel issues and will be based on before-and-after comparison of the personnel data, using both quantitative and qualitative criteria."[b] **Exit strategy.** See *Federal Register.*
Measurement approach	An attitude survey, structured interviews, and focus groups will be conducted to measure perceived organizational flexibility and perceived time savings from reduced administrative workload, employee perceptions of advancement, pay satisfaction, internal and external equity, perceived motivational power, fairness of awards, pay-contribution link, fairness of ratings, trust in supervisors, and adequacy of performance feedback. Workforce data will be collected on starting salaries of banded versus nonbanded employees; progression of new hires over time by band, career path; mean salaries by band, career path, demographics; total payroll cost; number of employees at high grade salaries pre- and post-banding; amount and number of awards by career path, pay-contribution correlations, turnover by contribution assessment.

[a]Laboratory Personnel Management Demonstration Project; Department of the Army, U.S. Medical Research and Materiel Command, Fort Detrick, Frederick, Md.; Notice, *Federal Register*, Vol. 63, No. 41, March 3, 1998, p. 10443.
[b]Laboratory Personnel Management, 1998, p. 10455.

Table A.10
Science and Technology Reinvention Laboratory Personnel Demonstration Project at the Army Missile Research, Development, and Engineering Center

Occupations	Civilian appropriate funded employees in the competitive and excepted service paid under the GS system. Scientific and Professional employees and positions will be included for employee development, performance appraisal, and award provisions only; their classification, staffing, and compensation will not change. SES, Federal Wage System employees, DA interns, and employees in the quality assurance specialist career program will not be covered.
Duration	1997 to present
Description	Established under the National Defense Authorization Act of FY 1995, which authorized the establishment of S&T Reinvention Laboratories in DoD. Designed by the Department of the Army "the purpose of this project is to demonstrate that the effectiveness of [DoD labs] can be enhanced by allowing greater managerial control over personnel functions and, at the same time, expanding the opportunities available to employees through a more responsive and flexible personnel system . . . [expected outcomes include:] (a) Increased quality in the total workforce and the products they produce; (b) increased timeliness of key personnel processes; (c) increased retention of high quality employees and increased non-retention of poor quality employees; and (d) increased satisfaction with MRDEC and its products by all customers it serves."[a] The project will introduce broad banding, a new classification system, a pay-for-performance management system, hiring and appointment authorities, expanded developmental opportunities for employees, and revised RIF procedures.
Experiment and analysis	The evaluation will be conducted by OPM's Personnel Resources and Development Center . . . selected parts of the evaluation will be completed using contractor support. . . . "An intervention impact model will be used to measure the effectiveness of the various personnel system changes or interventions . . . the main focus of the evaluation will be on the intermediate outcomes, i.e., the results specific personnel system changes which are expected to improve human resources management." "The ultimate outcomes are defined as improved organizational effectiveness, mission accomplishment, and customer satisfaction.

Exit strategy. See *Federal Register* for detailed conversion procedures.

Table A.10—(continued)

Measurement approach	An attitude survey, structured interviews, and focus groups will be conducted to measure: perceived organizational flexibility and perceived time savings from reduced administrative workload, employee perceptions of advancement, pay satisfaction, internal and external equity, perceived motivational power, fairness of awards, pay-contribution link, fairness of ratings, trust in supervisors, and adequacy of performance feedback. Workforce data will be collected on starting salaries of banded vs. non-banded employees; progression of new hires over time by band, career path; mean salaries by band, career path, demographics; total payroll cost; number of employees at high grade salaries pre and post banding; amount and number of awards by career path, pay-contribution correlations, turnover by contribution assessment.

[a]Science and Technology Reinvention Laboratory Personnel Demonstration Project at the Missile Research, Development, and Engineering Center (MRDEC); Notice, *Federal Register*, Vol. 62, No. 124, June 27, 1997, p. 34894.

Table A.11
Civilian Acquisition Workforce Personnel Demonstration Project

Occupations	DoD civilian acquisition workforce and all personnel assigned to support them. Limited to 95,000.
Duration	1999 to present
Description	The National Defense Authorization Act of FY 1996 authorized the establishment of a personnel demonstration project within the department's civilian acquisition workforce. "The purpose of the project is to enhance the quality, professionalism, and management of the workforce through improvements in the efficiency and effectiveness of the human resources management system."[a] Changes introduced include new hiring and appointment authorities, broad banding, simplified classification system created three occupation groups, contribution-based compensation and appraisal system, revised RIF procedures, enhanced professional development opportunities, and introduction of sabbaticals.
Experiment and analysis	The evaluation will be overseen by the Office of Merit Systems Oversight and Effectiveness in OPM, OSD (Acquisition and Technology); and the Office of the Deputy Assistant Secretary of Defense (Civilian Personnel Policy) . . . . "the evaluation approach uses an intervention impact model that specifies each personnel system change as an intervention, the expected effects of each intervention, the corresponding measure and the data source for obtaining the measures."[b]
Measurement approach	Attitude surveys: perceived flexibility in authority to hire, perceived time savings, pay-contribution correlation, perceived fairness of ratings, and so forth Personnel office data: offer-to-accept ratios, percent declinations, experience, education, skills, and so forth Workforce data: employee effectiveness; average length of employment, and so forth. "Baseline measures will be taken prior to project implementation. Then, repeated post-implementation measurement will be taken to allow longitudinal comparisons by intervention within and across DoD components. A comparison group will be selected and compared to the demonstration project group to determine the effects and outcomes of the project."*

[a]Civilian Acquisition Workforce Personnel Demonstration Project; Department of Defense; Notice, *Federal Register*, Vol. 64, No. 5, January 8, 1999, p. 1426.
[b]Civilian Acquisition Workforce, 1999, p. 1485.

Military Recruiting Experiments with RAND Participation

Table B.1
Enlistment Effects of the 2 + 2 + 4 Recruitment Experiment

Occupations	The eligible skills were those enlisted MOSs with lower than average rates of enlistment of high-quality recruits, relative to the Army's goals; AIT length less than 14 weeks; and gaps in the MOS widely distributed in reserve units across the country. 23 MOSs were included.[a]
Duration	15 months; July 1989–September 1990
Description	Study of an enlistment recruiting program for the U.S. Army designed to attract high-quality, college-bound youth in difficult recruiting times and to retain trained personnel by channeling them into the reserve force. The 2 + 2 + 4 Program expanded Army College Fund benefits to recruits who signed two-year contracts for active duty, noncombat occupational specialties plus two years in the reserves, and an additional four years in the Individual Ready Reserves.
Experiment and analysis	The Job-Offer Experiment: Army applicants were randomly assigned eligibility for the 2 + 2 + 4 Program through the Army's job reservation system, which allowed the researchers to estimate how eligibility for the program affected decisions about skill occupation and term of service. The Geographic Experiment tested whether there was true market expansion as a result of the program by looking at a set of geographical areas where the program was available to a random set of individuals, in comparison to a set of geographical areas where the program was available to every qualified applicant. The areas were matched on the following variables: (1) previous high-quality enlistment rates, (2) recruiting goals, (3) number of Army production recruiters, (4) civilian unemployment and wage rates, (5) population demographics. **Impact Analysis.** To examine both market expansion and skill and term-of-service effects, the study used a multivariate regression model to control for local economic conditions and unmeasured local factors (e.g., demographics, industrial structure, attitudes about military service, etc.) that may have had an impact on the recruiting success of the program.

Measurement approach	The counts of enlistment contracts were collected by month and by battalion throughout the experiment.
	Monthly data on unemployment rates, wage rates, and weekly hours for states and metropolitan areas were collected from the Bureau of Labor Statistics' *Employment and Earnings*.
Outcomes	The 2 + 2 + 4 Program was determined a success. It was shown to have expanded the market for high-quality recruits by 3%. The analysis also showed that the program did not significantly influence recruits to sign on for shorter terms of service than they would in the absence of the program but did influence recruits to go into hard-to-fill occupations.

SOURCE: Richard Buddin, *Enlistment Effects of the 2 + 2 + 4 Recruiting Experiment*, Santa Monica, Calif.: RAND Corporation, R-4097-A, 1991.
NOTE: Earlier draft reports include J. Michael Polich and Richard Buddin, *2 + 2 + 4 Recruiting Program: Test Design*, Santa Monica, Calif.: RAND Corporation, WD-4319-A, March 1989; and Richard Buddin, *2 + 2 + 4 Recruiting Program: Preliminary Enlistment Results*, Santa Monica, Calif.: RAND Corporation, WD-5205-A, November 1990.
[a]See Buddin, 1991, p. 18 for specifics.

Table B.2
Enlistment Effects and Policy Implications of the Educational Assistance Test Program

Occupations	Critical enlisted skill areas differed by service. The Navy primarily selected technical ratings to be included; the Army selected primarily combat arms MOSs; and the Air Force selected a mix.
Duration	10 months; December 1, 1980–September 30, 1981
Description	A large-scale experiment conducted by DoD, involving all of the services, to observe the effect of increases in educational benefits granted to recruits on the rate of enlistment.
Experiment and analysis	The study was designed to determine how effective three test programs with different educational benefit incentives were at increasing the enlistment rate among critical skill occupations in the Army, Navy, and Air Force. The experiment included a control group that received the status quo and three other groups that received varying levels of increased benefits in addition to the Veteran's Educational Assistance Program (VEAP) benefits.[a] **Impact Analysis.** To determine the effects of increased educational benefits on enlistments, the authors compared the three test groups with the control group on the gains in enlistment of high-quality recruits between a one-year base period and the test period. The authors also developed a regression model to control for variables that may impact enlistments, including local labor market conditions and recruiters' effort.
Measurement approach	**Enlistments:** from the Defense Manpower Data Center (DMDC), records of individual enlistment contracts during FY 1981, from which the authors generated counts of enlistments by Armed Forces Entrance and Examining Stations (AFEES) areas and month. **Youth population:** a special data tape prepared by the Census Bureau yielded estimates of youth populations by county. **Civilian labor market conditions:** average hourly earnings of production workers on manufacturing payrolls, average weekly hours, total nonagricultural employment, and the unemployment rate data were provided by the Bureau of Labor Statistics' *Employment and Earnings*. **Recruiting effort:** numbers of production recruiters fielded by each of the services, reported quarterly.
Outcomes	Each of the test programs increased enlistments of high-quality recruits in at least one of the services compared to the control group. The results also showed that the programs effectively channeled recruits into eligible occupations in the Army and Air Force.

SOURCE: Richard Fernandez, *Enlistment Effects and Policy Implications of the Educational Assistance Test Program*, Santa Monica, Calif.: RAND Corporation, R-2935-MRAL, 1982.

[a]The less generous VEAP took the place of the GI Bill in 1976.

Table B.3
College First/GED Plus National Recruiting Test: Year 1 Report

Occupations	All enlisted MOSs
Duration	5 years; 2000–2005
Description	In response to recruiting challenges faced by the Army, RAND designed pilot recruiting programs to target two markets previously untapped by traditional recruiting and is evaluating their effects on recruitment. College First is aimed at high-quality young adults interested in enrolling in two-year colleges or vocational schools, before entering active duty. The program offers recruits a stipend, college loan repayment, a cash bonus, and rank of E4 upon entering active duty. GED Plus is aimed at high-quality recruits lacking a high school diploma by offering an opportunity to obtain their general education diploma (GED).
Experiment and analysis	The performance of the two pilot programs was assessed across a balanced set of geographic areas and a number of other dimensions, including previous recruiting production of the area, demographic characteristics, and economic characteristics. The evaluation included five tests cells: one control group, two College First cells, and two GED Plus cells. Program characteristics were varied slightly in the two cells for each of the programs. The study authors have completed the first year of data collection and analysis and will continue to assess the impact of the programs into a second year. The analysis will compare the impact of the two programs on market expansion for recruits as well as substitution effects. To do this the authors are comparing the performance in the test cells since the beginning of the experiment with how the same battalions performed in the 12 months before the program started, compared with the performance of the control cell in the same time periods.
Measurement approach	The following data are being collected: **Previous recruiting production:** total number of recruits, number of graduate-senior high-aptitude contracts **Current missions and quotas:** number of on-production recruiters and advertising dollars **Demographic and economic characteristics:** size of youth population, race and ethnic makeup, unemployment rate, per capita income, and average weekly wages **Educational attainment:** percentage of high school dropouts, high school graduates, junior college attendees, and four-year college attendees Army National Guard funding for college available in the area
Outcomes	The early results of this experiment are promising—both College First and GED Plus are increasing the college market of recruits. However, the expansion is not occurring in the high-quality segment of the recruit population.

SOURCE: Orvis 2001.

Table B.4
Enlistment Bonus Experiment

Occupations	Enlisted MOSs, primarily combat specialties such as infantry, armor, and artillery
Duration	23 months; July 1982–June 1984
Description	Study of the Enlistment Bonus Experiment, resulting from the passage of the Uniformed Services Pay Act in 1981, which allowed services to pay larger cash bonuses to enlisted members upon signing up for duty
Experiment and analysis	The experiment tested two bonus programs; one increased the bonus for a four-year enlistment and the other introduced a bonus for a three-year enlistment, plus a control group that received the regular bonus offered. The three programs were randomly assigned to different geographic areas and balanced on a number of factors, including previous enlistment rates, economic conditions, and demographics.
	The impact analysis was designed to quantify effects of the bonus on market expansion, skill channeling, and term of enlistment, using a multivariate simultaneous equations model that compares year-to-year changes in monthly enlistment totals between the test and control groups, adjusting for demographics of different areas, changes in attitudes toward military services, and so forth.
Implementation and measurement approach	Army recruiters and job counselors disseminated bonus program information. Recruiting guides and manuals were updated to provide information about the new bonuses. DoD conducted a survey in the spring of 1983 asking a representative sample of military service applicants whether their recruiter had discussed the program with them.
	The Army also had its advertising agency put together kits for recruiters to help them advertise the bonuses through the local media and directly to the populations in their area. The researchers verified that each geographic area had advertised in their local area by examining all the local advertising purchases during the experiment, which showed that $400,000 a year was being spent on advertising the programs on average in each area.

The data collected for the experiment included counts of high- and low-quality enlistments by skill group and term of enlistment. Data on each of these variables were collected monthly for the duration of the experiment plus a one-year base period for each of the Military Entrance Processing Station areas.

In addition, data on the control variables that may have an impact on enlistment were collected:

- average unemployment rate and civilian wage rate: collected at the state level from the Bureau of Labor Statistics
- average number of recruiters on production: provided quarterly by areas covered by Army Recruiting Command battalions
- recruiter quotas: quotas for high- and low-quality recruits were reported quarterly by each battalion
- annual total expenditures on national and local advertising: obtained from N.W. Ayer, the Army's advertising agency.

Outcomes   The analysis of the market expansion effect showed that the bonus programs would increase the number of high-quality Army recruits, holding all other factors constant. The analysis also showed that the bonus programs had significant effects on enlistees' skill and term of service choices. The programs channeled recruits into certain skills areas and into longer term of service contracts. The authors concluded that bonuses are a highly effective recruiting tool that offers the benefits of flexibility and effectiveness.

SOURCE: J. Michael Polich, James N. Dertouzos, and S. James Press, *The Enlistment Bonus Experiment*, Santa Monica, Calif.: RAND Corporation, R-3353-FMP, 1986.

Table B.5
The Multiple Option Recruiting Experiment

Occupations	Enlisted occupations, primarily combat arms specialties
Duration	12 months; 1979
Description	Study of the Multiple Option Recruiting Experiment (MORE) to determine whether different combinations of enlistment incentives would affect the enlistment rates of high-quality youth and the rates of recruitment into hard-to-fill skill areas in the Army, Navy, and Marine Corps
Experiment and analysis	Each service employed a different test of enlistment incentive combinations, which included a two-year term of enlistment, expanded postservice educational benefits, and an option permitting recruits to choose reserve duty in lieu of active military service after completing initial training.
	The impact analysis conducted by the authors examined the enlistment responses to the incentive options and the feasibility of adopting one or more of the enlistment incentives as part of the services' overall recruiting strategy. Enlistment gains of the test groups were compared to the control group between a one-year base period and the test period. The authors also employed a multiple regression model to control for other effects on enlistment, including changes in the unemployment rates, wage rates, and measures of recruiting effort.
Measurement approach	The following data were collected:
	Enlistment: from the DMDC, records of individual enlistment contracts were used to generate counts of enlistments for each AFEES area by service, sex, mental category, and educational attainment
	Unemployment rates and wage rates: Bureau of Labor Statistics' *Employment and Earnings* for each AFEES
	Recruiter manning levels: for the Army, data were obtained from the Army Recruiting Command; for the Navy, the director of the Research and Analysis Division in the Recruiting Command provided data; the Personnel Procurement Division provided the Marine Corps data.
Outcomes	The regression results supported the "raw" relative increases in enlistment rates of the test groups over the test period compared to the control group. Neither analysis revealed significant effects of any of the incentives. Most notably, the authors concluded that the experiment refuted the hypothesis that a shorter term of enlistment would attract large numbers of high-quality recruits into hard-to-fill occupations. Small gains in enlistment of certain kinds of recruits were seen with the educational benefit and reserve option, but neither was very large.

SOURCE: G. W. Haggstrom, Thomas J. Blaschke, Winston K. Chow, and William Lisowski, *The Multiple Option Recruiting Experiment*, Santa Monica, Calif.: RAND Corporation, R-2671-MRAL, 1981.

Legislation

Section 4703 of Title 5 (Government Organization and Employees) of United States Code allows the Office of Personnel Management (OPM) to conduct and evaluate demonstration projects that are not limited by the lack of specific authority under Title 5. Section 4703 outlines in detail what actions have to be taken in order to conduct a demonstration project. Section 9507 of Title 5 contains streamlined demonstration project authority and outlines procedures for the Secretary of the Treasury to implement demonstration projects for the Internal Revenue Service. Title 10 (Armed Forces) of United States Code provides no such general authority to conduct demonstration projects for military personnel.

In order to conduct a demonstration project of alternative career paths for military personnel, the Department of Defense (DoD) could proceed in two ways. One way would be to catalog in detail all of the authorities that would need to be waived in order to conduct the demonstration and then to seek the specific waivers from Congress. Among the difficulties in this approach is that DoD might not foresee a waiver that is ultimately needed, and assuming that the Congress would grant it, the omission could delay the demonstration project by up to a year. The second approach would be to seek broad authority for the Secretary of Defense to conduct demonstration projects along the lines of the authority granted to OPM and the Secretary of the Treasury by Title 5. This latter approach is the one we recommend. Language similar to that immediately below (which was developed in conjunction with the project sponsor) would allow needed authority.

Sec. _____. Demonstration Projects

(a) The Secretary of Defense may, directly or through agreement or contract with one or more agencies and other public and private organizations, conduct, evaluate, and terminate demonstration projects. Subject to the provisions of this section, the conducting of demonstration projects shall not be limited by any lack of specific authority under this title to take the action contemplated, or by any provision of this title or any rule or regulation prescribed under this title which is inconsistent with the action, including any law or regulation relating to

  (1) the methods of establishing qualification requirements for, recruitment for, and appointment to positions;

  (2) the methods of determining requirements and compensating personnel;

  (3) the methods of assigning, reassigning, or promoting personnel;

  (4) the methods of providing incentives to personnel, including the provision of group or individual incentive bonuses or pay;

  (5) the methods of involving military members in personnel decisions; and

  (6) the methods of reducing requirements.

(b) Before conducting or entering into any agreement or contract to conduct a demonstration project, the Office shall

  (1) develop a plan for such project that describes its purpose, the personnel groups to be covered, the project itself, its anticipated outcomes, and the method of evaluating the project;

  (2) provide notification of the proposed project, at least 30 days in advance of the date any project proposed under this section is to take effect

    (A) to personnel who are likely to be affected by the project; and

    (B) to each House of the Congress;

  (3) obtain approval from each Service and Defense Agency involved of the final version of the plan; and

  (4) provide each House of the Congress with the final version of the plan.

(c) No demonstration project under this section may provide for a waiver except with the approval of the Secretary of Defense.

(d)

(1) Each demonstration project shall

   (A) involve not more than 5,000 individuals other than individuals in any control groups necessary to validate the results of the project; and

   (B) terminate before the end of the five-year period beginning on the date on which the project takes effect, except that the project may continue beyond the date to the extent necessary to validate the results of the project.

(2) Not more than ten active demonstration projects may be in effect at any time.

While we believe (subject of course to review by the military services and Office of General Counsel) that such language would be sufficient to allow for waivers of existing authority in order to test new policies, additional authority of a type that does not now exist may also be needed. For example, the concept of employability is introduced in several of the proposed demonstration projects and it will be necessary to determine if the authority to separate personnel on such a basis exists. One possible method for implementing this would be to allow involuntary, but not mandatory, separation at existing tenure points so that decisions about individual officers and not groups of them would be made. Moreover, if and when a demonstration project is terminated and not continued, the secretary will need authority to grandfather or otherwise provide relief, if needed, to participants. We suggest use of existing compensation authorities to include those of Title 37 as "workarounds" to conduct the test. Waived or changed Title 10 and Title 37 authority might also be needed to do this.

What provisions of Title 10 might in fact need to be waived in order to conduct demonstration projects of the type outlined in this report? While not claiming to be comprehensive, we believe that waivers of at least the following might be needed:

- Section 523: Authorized grade strengths
- Section 611: Convening of selection boards
- Section 627: Failure of selection for promotion
- Section 632: Effect of failure of selection for promotion
- Section 633 and 634: Retirement for years of service
- Section 1251: Retirement for age
- Section 1370: Retired grade commissioned officers.

Table C.1 aligns such waivers with each proposed demonstration. The table may not be comprehensive.

Table C.1
Suggested Waivers to Title 10

Proposed Demonstration Project	Section Title 10	Reason for and Effect of Waiver
Air Force-designated communities	632, 633, 634, 611	Section 632 mandates discharge or retirement if twice failed of selection to the next higher grade for O-3 and O-4. (Policy and/or law currently allow most to reach 20 YOS.) Section 633 mandates retirement for O-5 at 28 years of commissioned service. Waiver would allow certain O-4s and O-5s to serve for up to 30 YOS respectively without the convening of a selection board under Section 611(b). Alternatively, waiver of the procedures for statutory selection boards might accomplish the same purpose or changing the authority for such boards from Title 10 to regulations prescribed by the Secretary of Defense, which presumably would provide more flexibility in procedures.
Army-FAO	627	Section 627 designates officers below O-6 not selected for promotion as failed of selection for promotion. Waiver of 627 removes the failure stigma. Officers would remain continuously competitive for promotion. (Additional waiver to promotion procedures may be needed.)

Table C.1—(continued)

Proposed Demonstration Project	Section Title 10	Reason for and Effect of Waiver
	632, 633, 634	Section 632 mandates discharge or retirement if twice failed of selection to the next higher grade for O-3 and O-4. (Policy and/or law currently allow most to reach 20 YOS.) Section 633 mandates retirement for O-5 at 28 years of commissioned service and section 634 mandates retirement of O-6 at 30 YOS. Waiver would allow O-4, O-5, and O-6 to serve until statutory retirement age, currently 62 or approximately 40 YOS.
	523	Section 523 controls the distribution of officers in O-4, O-5, and O-6. If this distribution is fixed, promotion opportunity and flow points have to vary if officers serve longer in grade. Waiver would remove O-4 and O-5 constraints (would leave O-6) that would allow a greater likelihood of achieving policy goals for promotion opportunity and timing given longer careers.
Navy-SWO	632	Section 632 mandates discharge or retirement if twice failed of selection to the next higher grade for O-3 and O-4. (Policy and/or law currently allow most to reach 20 YOS.) Waiver would allow certain O-4s, to serve to 24 YOS without the convening of a selection board under Section 611(b).
	523	Section 523 controls the distribution of officers in O-4, O-5, and O-6. If this distribution is fixed, promotion opportunity and flow points have to vary if officers serve longer in grade. Waiver would remove O-4 in the program from the calculation and would allow a greater likelihood of achieving policy goals for promotion opportunity and timing given longer service.
	Multiple (or new authority)	Sections 3962 and 8962 allow retirement for higher grade for service in special positions and have narrow applicability. Waiver (or new authority) would allow officers in this program to be retired as an O-5 (if not previously promoted to O-5). Retirement pay would not be affected.

Table C.1—(continued)

Proposed Demonstration Project	Section Title 10	Reason for and Effect of Waiver
USMC-designated positions	632, 633, 634, 611	Section 632 mandates discharge or retirement if twice failed of selection to the next higher grade for O-3 and O-4. (Policy and/or law currently allow most to reach 20 YOS.) Section 633 mandates retirement for O-5 at 28 years of commissioned service and section 634 mandates retirement of O-6 at 30 YOS. Waiver would allow certain O-4s, O-5s, and O-6s to serve for 24, 32, and 34 YOS respectively without the convening of a selection board under Section 611(b). Alternatively, waiver of the procedures for statutory selection boards might accomplish the same purpose or changing the authority for such boards from Title 10 to regulations prescribed by the Secretary of Defense, which presumably would provide more flexibility in procedures.

Air Force Effective Manning

The Air Force effective manning can be calculated as the percentage of billets being filled by an officer with the appropriate grade and AFSC. Officer requirements are the sum of the number of officers in a single grade with a particular AFSC, plus the number of vacant billets in that grade for that AFSC. Filled billets are calculated as the number of officers in a single grade with a particular AFSC *minus* the number of vacant billets at the next lower grade.

These calculations make two assumptions. First, they assume all officers who are assigned in "non-core" duty AFSCs are appropriately assigned to meet needs of the Air Force. Therefore, a pilot with an engineering duty AFSC, for example, is assumed to be a pilot requirement. The calculations also assume that O-4s can fill company grade vacancies, O-5s can fill O-4 vacancies, and O-6s can fill O-5 vacancies.

Table D.1 is an example of effective manning calculation for pilots.

Table D.1
Air Force Calculation of Effective Manning

Grade	Requirements	Inventory	Filled Billets	Vacant Billets	Effective Manning
O-1–O-3	7,479	5,557	5,557	1,922	
O-4	2,480	2,987	2,987 – 1,922 = 1,065	2,480 – 1,065 = 1,415	1,065/2,480 = 43%
O-5	1,722	2,023	2,023 – 1,415 = 608	1,722 – 608 = 1,114	608/1,722 = 35%

SOURCE: Air Force Senior Leader Management Office.

Navy and Air Force Program Modeling

To calculate the impact of the policy packages in the affected Navy and Air Force communities, we calculated the expected man-years served by an entire cohort with and without the new policies. The calculations were generated using historical data to predict cohort size and continuation rates. The Navy data were provided by DMDC and covered the period 1987 to 2002; the Air Force data were provided by the Air Force Personnel Center and covered the period 1994 to 2002.

The calculations required several steps. We began by finding year-to-year continuation rates and average cohort sizes in each community. Using these parameters, we generated a cohort profile through 30 YOS, so that a cohort gradually diminishes as a result of separations, retirements, and promotions to general officer in later years. The starting point for Navy SWOs was the first year of service; for Air Force pilots the starting point was the twelfth YOS, which we chose because the pilot community has a large inflow of officers after year 1. The sum of the number of officers in a cohort each year equals the total man-years served by a cohort through 30 YOS.[1] With parameters based only on historical data, this number represents our baseline forecast absent any policy changes.

By making various changes to the cohort profile, we calculated a range of estimates for increased total man-years resulting from the proposed programs. We calculated ranges because we do not know what

---

[1] As a scaled-down example, if 100 officers serve in Year 1 and 75 stay to serve in Year 2, 50 stay to serve in Year 3, and 25 stay to serve in Year 4 before retiring, the total man-years served by the cohort is 100 + 75 + 50 + 25 = 250 years.

the participating officers would have done if the programs were not in place. If it turns out that the officers selected to participate would have served long careers anyway, the programs will have a negligible effect. If, on the other hand, the officers selected to participate would have soon left the communities, the program effect will be much larger. A middle-ground estimate assumes that the participating officers would be similar to the rest of their cohort with respect to continuation rates, that is, some would leave soon, some serve a few more years, and some serve as long as possible. The actual effect will probably be somewhat larger than the middle-ground estimate because continuation rates for an entire cohort include those officers who are highly competitive for promotion, and who, therefore, might be more likely to stay than officers who do not screen for XO or who are not selected for in-residence service school.

For the Navy program, we assumed that with the program in place all participants would continue to 24 years. To estimate the net effect of the program, our assumptions are as follows: For the low estimate, all participants would have served to 24 years even without the program. For the middle estimate, the ten SWOs chosen after the third XO screen otherwise would have had continuation rates similar to the entire community until 20 years, when we assume all retire. For the high estimate, the ten SWOs chosen after the third XO screen otherwise would have left the service immediately and the five chosen at 20 years would otherwise have retired at that point.

For the Air Force program, we assumed that with the program in place, all participants would continue to 30 years. To estimate the net effect of the program, our assumptions are as follows: For the low estimate, all O-4s would have served to 24 years and all O-5s would have served to 28 years even without the program. For the middle estimate, participants otherwise would have had continuation rates similar to the entire community, until 20 years when we assume all remaining O-4s retire or 24 years when we assume all remaining O-5s retire. For the high estimate, O-4s and O-5s otherwise would have left the service at 13 and 17 YOS, respectively.

There are several Air Force occupations that typically have effective manning shortages, but they have different career patterns, promotion opportunities, and so forth, which makes modeling the effects of a single program difficult. We focus our analysis on pilots because they are expected to have effective manning shortages for years to come and are the largest of the occupations that would likely be affected. Of the five occupations identified with large effective manning shortages—pilots, development engineers, scientists, manpower, and public affairs—pilots represent about 75 percent of the total, so we assume that about 20 of the 25 O-4s and 15 of the 20 O-5s selected for participation will be pilots.

Table E.1
Impact on Navy Surface Warfare Community

YOS	Yr.-to-Yr. Contin. %	Cohort Size	Participants	Participant Career Pattern Without Program		
				Low Estimate	Middle Estimate	High Estimate
1	100	900.0				
2	100	900.0				
3	100	900.0				
4	92	829.4				
5	83	689.5				
6	79	544.4				
7	78	426.5				
8	72	307.4				
9	77	235.7				
10	86	203.1				
11	90	181.8				
12	86	156.3				
13	85	132.3				
14	90	119.0				
15	93	110.1	10.0	10.0	10.0	0.0
16	90	98.7	10.0	10.0	8.5	0.0
17	91	90.0	10.0	10.0	7.6	0.0
18	100	90.0	10.0	10.0	7.0	0.0
19	100	90.0	10.0	10.0	6.3	0.0
20	100	90.0	10.0	10.0	5.8	0.0
21	50	45.0	15.0	15.0	0.0	0.0
22	90	40.5	15.0	15.0	0.0	0.0
23	89	36.0	15.0	15.0	0.0	0.0
24	90	32.4	15.0	15.0	0.0	0.0
Total man-years		7248.2	120.0	120.0	45.2	0.0
Net increase in man-years (difference from column 4)				0.0	74.8	120.0
Percent increase in man-years (percent of column 3)				0.0%	1.0%	1.7%

Table E.2
Impact on Air Force Pilot Community

YOS	Yr.-to-Yr. contin. (%)	Cohort Size	Participants	Participant Career Pattern Without Program		
				Low Estimate	Middle Estimate	High Estimate
1						
2						
3						
4						
5						
6						
7						
8						
9						
10						
11						
12		600.0				
13	88	530.9	20.0	20.0	20.0	0.0
14	89	471.2	20.0	20.0	17.8	0.0
15	92	435.7	20.0	20.0	16.4	0.0
16	100	435.7	20.0	20.0	16.4	0.0
17	97	422.0	35.0	35.0	30.9	0.0
18	94	398.4	35.0	35.0	28.3	0.0
19	94	372.5	35.0	35.0	26.3	0.0
20	92	343.8	35.0	35.0	25.3	0.0
21	68	234.3	35.0	35.0	11.9	0.0
22	70	165.2	35.0	35.0	11.3	0.0
23	74	121.7	35.0	35.0	10.5	0.0
24	76	92.2	35.0	35.0	9.7	0.0
25	82	75.5	35.0	15.0	0.0	0.0
26	86	65.0	35.0	15.0	0.0	0.0
27	73	47.4	35.0	15.0	0.0	0.0
28	69	32.8	35.0	15.0	0.0	0.0
29	59	19.3	35.0	0.0	0.0	0.0
30	85	16.4	35.0	0.0	0.0	0.0
Total man-years		4880.6	570.0	420.0	224.8	0.0
Net increase in man-years (difference from column 4)				150.0	345.2	570.0
Percent. increase in man-years from YOS 12 to 30 (percent of column 3)				3.1%	7.1%	11.7%

Bibliography

The Army Training and Leader Development Panel Officer Study Report to the Army, Washington, D.C., May 2001.

Buddin, Richard. *2 + 2 + 4 Recruiting Program: Preliminary Enlistment Results,* Santa Monica, Calif.: RAND Corporation, WD-5205-A, November 1990.

———, *Enlistment Effects of the 2 + 2 + 4 Recruiting Experiment,* Santa Monica, Calif.: RAND Corporation, R-4097-A, 1991.

Buddin, Richard, and J. Michael Polich, *The 2 + 2 + 4 Recruiting Experiment: Design and Initial Results,* Santa Monica, Calif.: RAND Corporation, N-3187-A, 1990.

Civilian Acquisition Workforce Personnel Demonstration Project; Department of Defense; Notice, *Federal Register,* Vol. 64, No. 5, January 8, 1999, pp. 1425–1492.

Cook, T. D., and D. T. Campbell, *Quasi-experimentation: Design and Analysis for Field Settings,* Chicago: Rand McNally, 1979.

Cook, T. D., D. T. Campbell, and L. Peracchio, "Quasi Experimentation," in M. D. Dunnette and L. M. Hough, eds., *Handbook of Industrial and Organizational Psychology*: Vol. 1, Palo Alto, Calif.: Consulting Psychologists Press, Inc., 1990.

Defense Manpower Commission, *Defense Manpower: The Keystone of National Security, Report to the President and the Congress,* Washington, D.C., March 1976.

Dillender, Mike, Marshall Pattie, Allison Rohrer, and Angela Shaw, "Give Officers a New Option," *Navy Proceedings,* October 2002, pp. 46–47.

Fernandez, Richard, *Enlistment Effects and Policy Implications of the Educational Assistance Test Program*, Santa Monica, Calif.: RAND Corporation, R-2935-MRAL, 1982.

Haggstrom, G. W., Thomas J. Blaschke, Winston K. Chow, and William Lisowski, *The Multiple Option Recruiting Experiment*, Santa Monica, Calif.: RAND Corporation, R-2671-MRAL, 1981.

Jumper, John (Air Force Chief of Staff), "Chief's Sight Picture," November 6, 2002.

Laboratory Personnel Management Demonstration Project; Department of the Air Force; Notice, *Federal Register*, Vol. 61, No. 230, November 27, 1996, pp. 60399–60424.

Laboratory Personnel Management Demonstration Project; Department of the Army, U.S. Medical Research and Materiel Command, Fort Detrick, Frederick, Md.; Notice, *Federal Register*, Vol. 63, No. 41, March 3, 1998, pp. 10439–10462.

Maze, Rick, "Rumsfeld Broaches Changes in Career Structures," *Army Times*, February 3, 2003, p. 12.

Naval Personnel Task Force, *A Strategic Human Resource Management System for the 21st Century*: Vol. I, Washington, D.C., September 2000.

Naval Sea Systems Command Warfare Centers Demonstration Project Web site, http://www.nswc.navy.mil/P/DEMO/ (as of June 3, 2003).

Orvis, Bruce R., James R. Hosek, and Michael G. Mattock, *PACER SHARE: Productivity and Personnel Management Demonstration Baseline Evaluation*, Santa Monica, Calif.: RAND Corporation, R-3753-FMP, 1990.

———, *PACER SHARE: Productivity and Personnel Management Demonstration, Third Year Evaluation*, Santa Monica, Calif.: RAND Corporation, MR-310-P&R, 1993.

Pogue, Forrest C., *George C. Marshall: Ordeal and Hope*, New York: Viking Press, 1966.

Polich, J. Michael, and R. Buddin, *2 + 2 + 4 Recruiting Program: Test Design*, Santa Monica, Calif.: RAND Corporation, WD-4319-A, March 1989.

Polich, J. Michael, James N. Dertouzos, and S. James Press, *The Enlistment Bonus Experiment*, Santa Monica, Calif.: RAND Corporation, R-3353-FMP, 1986.

Research and Demonstration Branch, Office of Performance Management, Office of Personnel Management, *Evaluation of the Navy Personnel Management Demonstration Project: Analysis of Survey and Interview Results 1979–1983,* Management Report II, July 1984.

Rossi, Peter H., Howard E. Freeman, and Mark W. Lipsey, *Evaluation: A Systematic Approach,* Thousand Oaks, Calif.: Sage Publications, 1999.

Schmitt, Nicholas J., "The 'Up-or-Out' Policy," *Navy Proceedings,* December 1979, pp. 35–40.

Science and Technology Reinvention Laboratory Personnel Demonstration Project at the Aviation Research, Development, and Engineering Center; Notice, *Federal Register,* Vol. 62, No. 124, June 27, 1997, pp. 34905–34932.

Science and Technology Reinvention Laboratory Personnel Demonstration Project at the Missile Research, Development, and Engineering Center (MRDEC); Notice, *Federal Register,* Vol. 62, No. 124, June 27, 1997, pp. 34875–34903.

Science and Technology Reinvention Laboratory Personnel Demonstration Project at the U.S. Army Research Laboratory (ARL); Notice, *Federal Register,* Vol. 63, No. 42, March 4, 1998, pp. 10679–10711.

Science and Technology Reinvention Laboratory Personnel Demonstration Project Final Plan: U.S. Army Engineer Waterways Experiment Station (WES), Vicksburg, Miss.; Notice; Republication, *Federal Register,* Vol. 63, No. 57, March 25, 1998, pp. 14579–14599.

Surface Warfare Officer Junior Officer Survey, 1999 and 2001.

United States Code, Title 5, Section 4703, Demonstration Projects.

———, Title 5, Section 9507, Streamlined Demonstration Project Authority.

———, Title 10, Section 523, Authorized Strengths.

———, Title 10, Section 611, Convening of Selection Boards.

———, Title 10, Section 627, Failure of Selection for Promotion.

———, Title 10, Section 632, Effect of Failure of Selection for Promotion.

———, Title 10, Section 633, Retirement for Years of Service: Regular Lieutenant Colonels and Commanders.

———, Title 10, Section 634, Retirement for Years of Service: Regular Colonels and Captains.

————, Title 10, Section 1251, Age 62: Regular Commissioned Officers; Exceptions [for retirement for age].

————, Title 10, Section 1370, Commissioned Officers: General Rule; Exceptions [for retired grade].

————, Title 10, Section 3962, Higher Grade for Service in Special Positions.

The U.S. Commission on National Security/21st Century, *Road Map for National Security: Imperative for Change,* February 2001.

U.S. Naval Research Laboratory (NRL) Personnel Management Demonstration Project; Department of the Navy (DON), Washington D.C.; Notice, *Federal Register,* Vol. 64, No. 121, June 24, 1999, pp. 33969–34046.

U.S. Office of Personnel Management Demonstration Projects Evaluation Handbook, www.opm.gov/demos/resources.asp (as of April 1, 1999).

U.S. Senate, Committee on Armed Services, *Officer Personnel Act of 1947,* Hearings 80th Congress, 1st Session, July 16, 1947.

Vandergriff, Donald, *The Path to Victory: America's Army and the Revolution in Human Affairs,* Novato, Calif.: Presidio Press, 2002.